Cowboy Princess

Cowboy Princess

Life with My Parents—
Roy Rogers and Dale Evans

Cheryl Rogers-Barnett and Frank Thompson

Taylor Trade Publishing
Lanham • New York • Toronto • Oxford

Published by Taylor Trade Publishing
An imprint of The Rowman & Littlefield Publishing Group, Inc.
4501 Forbes Boulevard, Suite 200
Lanham, Maryland 20706

Distributed by National Book Network

Library of Congress Cataloging-in-Publication Data
Thompson, Frank T., 1952–
    Cowboy princess : life with my parents, Roy Roger and Dale Evans /
Frank Thompson and Cheryl Rogers-Barnett.
        p. cm.
    ISBN 1-58979-026-X (hard. : alk. paper)
    1. Rogers, Roy, 1911– 2. Rogers, Dale Evans. 3. Actors—United
States—Biography. 4. Singers—United States—Biography. 5.
Rogers-Barnett, Cheryl, 1940– I. Rogers-Barnett, Cheryl, 1940– II.
Title.
    PN2287 .R73 T48 2003
    790.2'0922—dc21

                                                2003012642

⊗™ The paper used in this publication meets the minimum requirements of
American National Standard for Information Sciences—Permanence of Paper for
Printed Library Materials, ANSI/NISO Z39.48–1992.
Manufactured in the United States of America.

To my Mom, Dale Evans Rogers—Queen of the West
. . . and my wonderful husband, Larry
Without them, this book never would have been written

Contents

Acknowledgments

As **Larry** and I travel around the country, representing the museum and Mom and Dad's heritage, people invariably want to talk to me about what it was like growing up in our household. They all seem to enjoy my stories and more than a few of them were almost adamant that I put them in a book. I never thought I had enough interesting stories to fill a book. As a result, I never took their urgings seriously.

Mom did though. She wrote the foreword to the book, I am convinced, to add her encouragement and not just a little bit of pressure. The fact that she did this just three weeks prior to her passing put it in a light that almost made writing this book a mandate.

This is for you, Mom, for all you have meant to me, for all you have done for me and the rest of the world, as well.

And, to Larry. You never stopped urging me to write this book, constantly reminding me that Mom wanted me to. Without your persistence and your support, it never would have gotten done. Thanks, Honey.

I am grateful to Frank Thompson who gently and patiently led me back through memories long forgotten. And to his talented wife, Claire McCulloch Thompson, who graciously and lovingly supported Frank as he collaborated with me. Mike Emmerich, our editor at Taylor, gets a special thanks for taking a chance on an unpublished author. Boyd Magers, my boss at Western Clippings, was kind enough to share his considerable archival knowledge in helping us to be as historically accurate as possible. It was so much fun talking to Corky Randall about Trigger. Thanks to Patrick Curtis for helping me relive the Republic days. Thanks to Nina Dilbeck for scanning in and touching up my photos.

To Judy Kelly Whisenant and Joanne Hitz, I am very appreciative of the long, long friendship we share and the opportunity to reminisce about some fun and not-so-fun times. Judy was especially valuable since she was really a surrogate member of our family; she offered some great insights.

Our friends Charles and Laverne Thompson have always offered friendship and encouragement—and refuge as well. Thank you for everything.

I am deeply grateful to Leonard Maltin and his dear wife Alice. Leonard is a wonderful friend who always believed that I had a story to tell, and encouraged me to tell it. It was Leonard who put me together with Frank Thompson, so he is very directly responsible for this book in so many ways.

There are two people who, with their friendship and support, have made possible the successes we have had over the last five years. Jim and Beverly Rogers of Sunbelt Communication have meant more to us, the family in general, the museum and especially to Mom, than anyone will likely know. They provided the basis for Mom to keep active and productive in her last years by seeing to it that she was able to attend the Lone Pine Film Festival and The Festival of the West where she conducted book signings of her last book, *Rainbow on a Hard Trail*. Their efforts helped raise the quality of life in her last years. And to us, they have single-handedly allowed us to travel around the country, in the Royrogersmobile, promoting and perpetuating the legacy of Mom and Dad to new and old fans, alike. We are grateful beyond words for this rare and invaluable friendship. Thank you, Jim and Beverly.

Cheryl Rogers-Barnett

Foreword

$\mathcal{I}$ **am delighted** that Cheryl has accepted the urging and encouragement to write the book about what it was like growing up in our household. Cheryl, since she was the first of Roy's children, has some wonderful recollections of the early years when her father was becoming the No. 1 box office draw and King of the Cowboys. She also remembers the tragedies.

Cheryl couldn't have been more than two or three years old when I first met her. Roy would often bring her to the Republic Studios with him in the morning and the lot would become her playground. She used to head straight for my dressing room and into my makeup. This was about the time that Roy and I were making our first picture together, *The Cowboy and the Señorita*. I distinctly remember how pretty she was and how much she reminded me of Shirley Temple. I thought she should have been my daughter, the one I always wanted to complement my son, Tom. How ironic that this thought would be realized in just a few short years when Roy and I would marry a year after his wife, Arline, passed away.

Cheryl and I have had some interesting times. I understood her precociousness, for she was so like me in a number of respects. That was as good as it was bad for both of us! But through it all, Cheryl was the one I depended upon, the one who was my support and strength when we lost Robin, Debbie and Sandy. While each one of our children is unique and precious, I don't know what I would do without Cheryl. Even today, she is my right arm and assists me in running my household and taking care of my medical needs, no small feat in itself. With all this, she still makes time to represent the museum and the family at public functions and film festivals, and sits on the Executive Committee of the Motion Picture and Television Fund's Golden Boot Awards and the Jim and Beverly Rogers Lone Pine Museum of Film History while serving as a Commissioner for The San Bernardino County Museum.

Her sunny disposition has been a blessing to us all. May God continue to keep and bless her.

Dale Evans Rogers
January 15, 2001

Introduction

e was the King of the Cowboys. She was the Queen of the West. They were the heroes of boys and girls everywhere who thrilled to their exploits in the movies or on TV and who grew up humming their theme song, "Happy Trails."

They were heroes to me, too. But they were also my Mom and Dad.

Today, the kids who loved and admired my parents are grown and have children—and grandchildren—of their own. But their love for Roy Rogers and Dale Evans has never dimmed, and neither has their interest in the exciting, sometimes tragic and often hilarious lives they led. As their oldest daughter, I have a unique perspective from which to tell that story. I practically grew up on the Republic Studios lot where Mom and Dad made their great movies. I remember, as a little girl, rehearsals with the original Sons of the Pioneers. I was aware of Mom and Dad as celebrities, but I also knew them as loving parents to a large and very diverse family. I shared their joy when they received honors and fame, and wept with them through the tragic loss of three of my siblings. Through it all, they remained in private what all of their fans believed them to be—honest, straightforward, loving people who gave freely of themselves and lived lives of adventure and humor—especially humor.

Dad was voted the number one box office cowboy star eleven times during the 1940s and 1950s. It was difficult for him to go out in public without being mobbed. He wasn't able to attend our school events and it was almost as hard for Mom. During those years it was almost impossible to find a movie magazine that did not have a story about the Rogers family. Reporters and flash-bulbs were everywhere and it seemed as though everyone was interested in our family.

Raising such a diverse family—we were our own mini-United Nations, and there was a twenty-six-year age span from oldest brother to youngest sister—had to be very tough for Mom and Dad. However, they tried to make sure that we lived completely normal lives—or as normal as possible. We all had our chores to do and we all knew the rules of the house. We received an allowance for cleaning our rooms, doing our homework and making passing grades—and we soon learned that breaking the rules would bring swift retribution.

As teenagers, we were provided with the basics plus a little extra. However, if we wanted a car or more trendy clothes, records or makeup, we were told the way to get them was to get a job. Mom and Dad taught by example—work hard, tell the truth, and avoid situations or places that would reflect badly on the family. In other words, we were taught to be responsible for our own actions, to put God first, then family, then country. We were raised with love and discipline.

I think that probably each one of my siblings could write a book—and every one would be completely different—our ages are spread out so much and our experiences were so varied. I was adopted as an infant, as was Dodie, but Mimi was thirteen and a half when she came here from Scotland. Tom Fox, Mom's son, was already in college when Mom and Dad married. Sandy was almost four years old when they found him in a home for handicapped children, and he had been abused as an infant. Debbie was a war orphan from Korea who came to us when she was four. I am sure that we all saw events that took place in the family from totally different perspectives and all would describe what happened in a different way. When we get together and reminisce, we laugh about that very thing.

But this book—partly my story, and partly the story of my beloved parents—is written from a point of view that is uniquely mine. I'll tell it in roughly chronological order, but don't expect a dry, straightforward autobiography in these pages. Instead, I look at *Cowboy Princess* as a collection of my memories, as one friend might share them with another.

More important, I want this book to be an up-close and personal introduction to the Queen of the West and the King of the Cowboys—otherwise known as my Mom and Dad. You'll learn some things about their private lives that might surprise you—hilarious things, and heartbreaking things And I think you'll learn—as everyone who ever met them learned—that their personalities offscreen were pretty much the same as their characters onscreen. They were honest, unpretentious, fun-loving, warm—and just a little eccentric. They were the most wonderful parents I could ever have wanted. And despite the sad times—and there were plenty of them—life with Roy Rogers and Dale Evans was mostly like riding along the happiest of happy trails.

Dad and Mommy Arline

Virtually all of my life I have repeatedly been asked these questions:

1. What is it like to be Roy Rogers and Dale Evans' daughter?
2. What are your parents *really* like?
3. Did you ever get to ride Trigger?
4. How many kids are there in your family?
5. Are you one of the adopted kids or are you really theirs?

In this book I'll answer all those questions and more, starting with the last one.

I can't remember a time when I didn't know that I had been adopted. Dad and Mommy (Mommy Arline) told me as soon as I was old enough to understand anything. They explained lovingly that they chose me very carefully—that I had been picked out of a whole room full of babies in Dallas, Texas. Dad always made sure that I understood that adoption was very special, an act of deepest love.

Since Dad always made a point of saying that he had chosen me out of a room full of babies, and as Mom said in the foreword to this book, "I thought she should have been my daughter," I felt

I couldn't be more "theirs." As a result, I don't remember ever having any problems with being adopted. To the contrary, it always made me feel special.

Mom (Dale) always loved to tell this story: When my sister Linda Lou and I would get into fights as kids, Linda would say "You're not really their daughter!" I would calmly reply, "No, they chose me and they got *stuck* with you!"

My story had its real beginning when Dad was born Leonard Slye in Cincinnati, Ohio, on November 5, 1911, and moved to a little rural community called Duck Run when he was about seven. Duck Run can't even be found on most Ohio maps although it's close to Portsmouth, Ohio, which is on the Kentucky border. His father worked in a shoe factory in Portsmouth but Dad later told a *Saturday Evening Post* reporter, "I didn't wear any shoes at all until I was about grown. The bottoms of my feet were like elephant hide!"

Duck Run, Ohio, was little more than a wide spot in the road—maybe forty people lived there at the time. In fact, when we made our only trip back there as a family in 1956, I think there were still only about forty inhabitants.

Dad's family was extremely poor. They didn't have a radio, but they did have an old crank Victrola that played cylinder recordings. Dad's favorite recordings were some Swiss yodels; he listened to them, tried it himself and found that he had a natural ability to yodel. In fact, he was pretty close to a musical genius. I don't think there was any kind of musical instrument that he couldn't play if he put his mind to it. Living out there in the middle of nowhere, always struggling just to survive, music became very important to the entire Slye family. They all sang and played something; they had to provide their own entertainment since they couldn't get it from the outside.

A lot has been written about Dad's career and how he got started in show business. A lot of it is accurate, a lot of it was studio hype, a lot of the later stories were based on such hype, and a lot of it is just plain wrong. For instance, on more than one occasion I have been approached by someone whose father/ uncle/cousin worked with Dad at a cannery/mine/store where Dad had been let go because all he did was sit around and play a guitar. Dad never held any such jobs and didn't own a guitar until after he came to Los Angeles and started getting work with local bands. People have also told me that they remember Dad picking and singing in the camps of migrant fruit pickers during the late '20s and early '30s. I don't remember Dad talking about this but it *might* have happened—that's how the Slye family entertained themselves. And Dad continued that practice for the rest of his life. Whenever we were anywhere music was being played informally, Dad would borrow a guitar, or other instrument, and join right in.

If Dad ever had any specific career ambition, I don't recall his ever talking about it. I think he was too concerned about where he and his family were going to get their next meal. According to Dad, his career just happened. He always said that he was where he was supposed to be, doing what he was meant to do—because his whole career was so improbable. That was the only explanation that made sense to him.

When Dad was about eighteen, the Great Depression hit. Grampy and Dad lost their jobs at the local shoe factory when it closed and they couldn't find anything else in the area. Dad's oldest sister was living in California and suggested that the family try their luck where the climate was better. Dad never was a fan of either cold or snow, so he and Grampy headed out to sunny California. Once there, they made a living picking fruit and Dad eventually got a job driving a gravel truck.

Dad's sister loved his playing and singing. She cajoled, teased, and pushed him into going on a local radio talent show. Since he was so shy, I can hardly believe that he got up the courage to do it, but I can imagine my Aunt Mary pushing him onto the stage. The audience liked his singing as well as his looks, and before he knew it, other opportunities to perform began to come his way.

One of Dad's first musical heroes was Jimmie Rodgers; he was fascinated by Rodgers's yodel. And when Dad formed the Sons of the Pioneers, the yodel was an important part of the unique sound that they created. Western music came to be identified by yodeling and the close harmony that characterized the singing style of Dad,

Bob Nolan, and Tim Spencer. All of them had worked with different groups, usually as singing duos. But when they finally came together to form The Pioneer Trio, they developed something different: yodeling in close three-part harmony the likes of which, it's pretty well agreed, no one had ever heard before. I think that this new sound formed the basis for their success because it was so different.

Before the formation of the Sons of the Pioneers, Dad played with a number of bands, such as the O Bar O Cowboys, the Rocky Mountaineers, the Texas Outlaws, the International Cowboys, and the Gold Star Rangers. Of course, he only got paid something like $5 for each appearance, so he would try to be on two or three radio shows every day, performing on each program under a different group name—but some days no one needed an extra musician. He met and performed with Bob Nolan and Tim Spencer at different times and with different groups. Bob and Tim had also worked with each other but not at the same time they worked with Dad.

Finally, Dad, Bob, and Tim formed The Pioneer Trio. Hugh and Karl Farr were added later and, as the Sons of the Pioneers, the group started making Western music history. Bob and Tim could write songs that made you feel as if you were on the prairie, could see the "Tumbling Tumbleweeds" or hear the "Cool Water" flowing, and when they sang about these things in their three-part harmony and yodeling, it was pure magic.

(There are three books I would recommend if you are interested in learning more about Dad's start in show business and the forming of the Sons of the Pioneers. They are Douglas B. Green's *Singing in the Saddle*; Bill O'Neal and Fred Goodwin's *The Sons of the Pioneers*; and the now-out-of-print *Hear My Song: the Story of the Celebrated Sons of the Pioneers,* written and updated by Ken Griffis.)

While with the O Bar O Cowboys in 1933, Dad and Tim left on a personal appearance tour of radio stations throughout Arizona, New Mexico, and Texas. The tour was great for exposure, but a total bust financially—in fact, Dad said they were out of money almost from the get-go. He loved telling the story about the little gimmick that they would use to get free food—and sometimes to meet girls. When they would be performing on the radio, Tim would say something like, "Oh gee, it is so tough being away from home and, boy, do we miss home cooking!" He would go on that they had been on the road and he was so tired of hotel food and that his favorite thing was fried chicken. One of the other guys would chime in, "Oh yeah, Tim, fried chicken is great, but you know what I really miss? Mashed potatoes and gravy." Then Dad would say how much he missed lemon meringue pie and how it beat all those other foods. This ploy almost always worked. Some young lady—and often more than one—would show up at the station with fried chicken or potatoes and gravy, or maybe even an invitation to dinner.

In Roswell, New Mexico, the young woman who turned up with *two* lemon meringue pies was Arline Wilkins. Dad was immediately attracted to Arline—and it wasn't just her cooking skills that he approved of. But there was a problem—Dad was married. When he was about twenty, Dad married a girl named Lucile Ascolese. He never told me much about her. Maybe he didn't remember much—the marriage lasted almost no time at all and according to Dad, they never lived together. But the marriage was still in effect when Dad met Arline and so their relationship didn't seem to have much of a future. But Arline's mother (my Nana) was ambitious and far more aggressive than Arline was. Nana decided to move to California with Arline and wait for Dad's marriage to be annulled, as he promised that it was going to be. On June 11, 1936, Dad and Arline were married.

Dad told me about a trip they took to New York in 1938 for the premiere of *Under Western Stars,* the first movie he starred in. They were staying at the Sherry Netherlands, a very swanky hotel. Dad and his agent left Mommy at the hotel for the day while they went off to a series of interviews and business meetings. When they got back to the hotel in the evening, they found that she had been sitting in the hotel room all day without anything to eat or drink, other than water. She had never been in a hotel room by herself and she just wasn't comfortable going downstairs and ordering in the restaurant by herself. She had no idea what room service was, and probably would have been afraid to order anything or open the door to the server, anyway. She was obviously terrified of the big city but even though it was years later when Dad told me the story, he still seemed mystified and somewhat upset with her. I wonder if his reaction wasn't a little bit out of guilt. After all, it hadn't been long since he was just a kid from Duck Run who wouldn't have known how to do these things either.

Mommy was a lady of classic beauty, as you can tell from her photographs. She was statuesque and almost everyone who spoke of Mommy would remark that she had the most beautiful hands they had ever seen. She had been raised to be a wife and mother; she cooked, she sewed, she made a home. She and my aunt were very artistic and would often paint together. She and her brother Don's wife, Aunt Neen, were really close. However, Mommy was also very introverted. She stuck to the house as much as possible and only had a couple of close friends—the actress Linda Hayes; Peggy Fisher, the wife of Shug Fisher of the Sons of the Pioneers; and our honorary aunt, Billie Betkijian. Except for these few friends, she wasn't very sociable; Mommy was a very quiet and reserved person.

I think Dad and his male friends really made her uncomfortable. The group that he ran with was made up of stuntmen and athletes, men of action who tended to be a bit on the loud and boisterous side. But those were the people he was always most comfortable with, the type of fellows he had grown up with in Duck Run. The music took care of his creative and professional needs, but otherwise he was a very physical outdoors type. Dad wasn't much of a reader, and I don't recall him having any quiet hobbies. Dad's thing was to be outdoors with his racing pigeons, or tramping around the mountains following coon hounds—that was his idea of heaven.

I have often wondered if Mommy and Daddy would have stayed together if she had lived. Even though they were very much in love, they were so very different that I don't see how they could have survived too many more years of the kinds of pressures that Hollywood puts on a marriage.

Our good friend Sue Anne Langdon has often wondered why I didn't marry an actor. I think the answer is, while there were a couple of actors that I went out with and really liked, I had already had enough of living in a fishbowl and didn't want to deal with the baggage that came with that lifestyle. After talking to some of Mommy's friends, I later came to feel that Mommy would have been much happier if she had stayed in Roswell where she knew everybody and they knew her. Hollywood seemed to intimidate her. My most lasting memories of Mommy aren't just of the love she showered on us, but also of how much she cried.

Like Dad, Mommy was very gifted musically; she was a fine pianist and had a lovely voice. She loved to play Irish songs, like her personal favorite, *Danny Boy*. She also played a lot of church music—her maternal grandfather had been a Methodist minister—and even some of the popular songs of the day. But although she played very well, I don't remember hearing that she ever wanted to perform in front of an audience. But Mommy often played and sang for us kids and sometimes Dad would join in. Those are some of my warmest memories of her and my early childhood.

I remember her best in the kitchen, cooking wonderful meals and letting me help. Whenever she prepared food it was like something you might see in a magazine; everything had to be pretty and look appetizing. Later on, that was a big change in our lives because most of the ladies who came to work for us were farm women—they just put the food in the bowl and sat it on the table without worrying about "presentation." But Mommy was quite artistic in everything she did. I remember her creating dishes that were like works of art. One I particularly remember is where she cut grapes in half and then made a cream cheese and nut filling. She would then put the filling in the center of a pear that had been halved and cored. Then she would let me carefully position the grapes on top of the cream cheese. Then she would place the pear on a lettuce leaf and sprinkle the dish with paprika. It looked like a still life painting when we were finished. And this wasn't for a fancy party either—it was one of our favorite dinner salads.

Every piece of linen in the house had hand embroidery or appliqué on it. She crocheted decorative edging on all the towels and sheets. Mommy made almost all of Linda Lou's and my dresses, trimming them with hand smocking and intricate embroidered details. Mommy was a very artistic and creative person and those were some of the ways in which she expressed herself.

I think one of the factors that led to Mommy's timidity was the fact that her mother, my Nana, had always been very protective of her only daughter. Nana had ambitions for her daughter to marry well, and Dad was the means to achieve those ambitions. Even though Dad was a struggling musician at the time, Nana always maintained that she knew he was going to be a big star one day.

She was used to controlling nearly every aspect of Mommy's life. Even though Mommy was in her late twenties when she and Dad met, she had never been on a date that my grandmother did not chaperone—not even with Dad. I think Nana was the one who was caught up in the show business mystique. I swear she must have read every movie magazine and listened to all of the popular gossip mavens such as Louella Parsons, Hedda Hopper, and Walter Winchell for the latest Hollywood news. Nana even wrote to and maintained a correspondence with Dad's fans, providing them with a lot of the details of our private lives.

As soon as she could arrange it, she got my grandfather to move to the San Fernando Valley, making him give up a well-established position in business and politics in Roswell. This really turned his life upside down. Once settled in nearby Van Nuys, Nana continued to exercise her control. Nana became the one who would plan the menu and do the shopping every time Mommy and Dad threw a party. Then she would come over and take charge of the preparations. It seemed my grandmother was always in the middle of everything. I always figured that Nana was the one who really wanted to come to Hollywood. She had all of the attributes of the typical stage mother.

After Dad and Mommy had been married for five or six years and she had had two or three miscarriages, her doctor told her that he didn't think she would ever be able to carry a child to term—and to continue trying would jeopardize her health. Despite this, Dad and Mommy really wanted a child, so they decided to look into adoption.

While Dad was on tour in Dallas, plugging his latest film, he visited a foundling home, Hope Cottage. Dad loved to tell the story of how he wiggled his fingers, made faces and funny noises to each baby. All the babies cried except one. I was the one who just reached up, grabbed his finger and cooed. According to Dad, right then, I stole his heart. He called Mommy back in California and said, "I found our baby!" I was six weeks old when Daddy first saw me. That first visit was brief, but as soon as he could, he returned to California to get Mommy, and together they returned to Dallas so she could meet me. Nana and Granddaddy came, too—it was sort of a committee decision, I think.

In those days, adoption was a pretty time-consuming activity— it wasn't like today when the adopting family can sometimes go right into the birthing room with the mother, with whom they have already made arrangements for the adoption. In 1940, by the time all the shots and physical checkups and paperwork had been cleared away, I was six months old. And that's when I finally arrived in California as the daughter of Roy and Arline Rogers. Yes, the name on my birth certificate is Cheryl Darlene Rogers.

When Dad was given a speaking part in a Gene Autry film as a bit of a bad guy, the studio didn't think that "Leonard Slye" would look good on a marquee—especially for a Western actor. So they changed his name to Dick Weston. That didn't last long though since, according to Dad, he "never felt like Dick Weston." When he got his first starring role in 1938's *Under Western Stars,* he changed his name to Roy Rogers, in tribute to Jimmie Rodgers and another of his heroes, Will Rogers. As for the first name, well, "Roy" just sounded good with Rogers and Dad liked the way the signature looked when he wrote it out. So, he worked all that out just in time—otherwise I would have been named Cheryl Slye.

It so often seems to happen that once a childless couple adopts, they suddenly become able to conceive. This is what happened to Dad and Mommy. Three years after I arrived, Mommy gave birth to my sister Linda Lou. And three years after that, Roy Jr. came along—the brother we've always called "Dusty."

When Linda Lou was a baby, and when Mommy was pregnant with Dusty, Dad took me to work with him at Republic Studios a lot. That was something I always enjoyed. Republic Studios was the greatest playground a kid could have.

Our day would start with breakfast at Du-Pars', a restaurant in Studio City that was practically across the street from Republic. They would see Dad coming and start preparing his pancakes with sides of mayonnaise and syrup. Yes, my dad put mayonnaise on his pancakes!

Years later, when I told this to my husband, Larry, he viewed me with some skepticism. It was only a short time later that we had occasion to go to breakfast with Mom and Dad. Sure enough, Dad ordered pancakes with a side of mayonnaise. He mentioned to Dad that I had told him the Du-Par's story but he had doubted me. Dad told him yes, it was true and was something he had started when he was just a boy and food was in short supply. He would put mayonnaise on half of his pancakes and call it dinner, the other half would get syrup and that became dessert. Now here he was, the King of the Cowboys, still taking comfort from that act.

The studio was fascinating. It was like a great big playground—exciting, fun, adventurous, and, best of all, safe. I couldn't get off the lot because there were guards everywhere and, anyway, they all knew me. Dad and I would walk through the gate in the morning and he would caution me, "Sissy, don't get dirty and don't get in trouble." Then off he would go to makeup and I would immediately head toward the horses and the stuntmen or go to the wardrobe or makeup departments. I soon learned the few rules: don't open a door that has a red light flashing; don't walk into a scene; and don't make noise after hearing, "All quiet on the set." Other than that, it was a freedom that I couldn't find anywhere else. What little girl wouldn't be enthralled by all of this? No wonder I would rather go to work with Dad than stay home with Mommy.

I have loved horses ever since Dad used to carry me on Trigger wrapped in a baby blanket. I had my own pony starting about the time that I learned to walk. The cowboys and wranglers were my friends and I would always make a beeline for the horses. The two cowboys I always looked for first were Ben Johnson and Richard

Farnsworth, with Harry Carey Jr. running a close third. Uncle Ben and Richard never seemed too busy to answer a child's questions or to sit me on a saddle between scenes. Of course, the fact that they were extremely handsome, kind young men didn't hurt either. I learned how to play gin rummy about the same time I learned to count; in other words, I don't remember not being able to play. Dad might not want me sitting in on the adult games on the set, but Uncle Ben and Richard would indulge the precocious four-year-old who knew her numbers—and, of course, in the beginning they also would coach me as to what card to play.

The other thing I loved about the studio was that I got to go to school with the "big" kids. Even when I was three and four, the studio's schoolteachers would let me sit in while they conducted classes for the studio's many child actors. Since there was usually only one teacher on a set, I was able to attend classes from kindergarten upwards and I really loved it. Of course, I wasn't being forced to attend, it was my choice! This was just one more game I could play.

When I talk to Bob Blake, Patrick Curtis or any of the other boys that grew up there at Republic, they all talk about the giant water tank and the caves—those were the things that the boys loved. But being a little girl, the wardrobe and the makeup departments—wow, that was Disneyland before there was a Disneyland! The dressers would let me play dress-up in some of the costumes, the makeup artists would put pancake, rouge, and lipstick on me, and the hairdressers put curls in my long hair. I just thought that was heaven; it was a wonderful place to be for a kid.

Then on the way home, we would stop at Sportsman's Lodge to catch trout for dinner. Even for Hollywood, this was an interesting restaurant, only a few blocks from our house on Longridge. They had trout ponds where you could catch your own fish for dinner, give them to the maitre d', and they would magically be returned to you, cleaned and ready to cook, in a small take-home box.

I was an active little kid—and I mean *really* active. Dad said that I never sat still and claimed that I must have had worms. When I had my oldest daughter, Lisa, she was a real handful and

Dad said that she reminded him a lot of me. Lisa was a very active, imaginative child who asked questions sixteen hours a day. She hardly ever napped, and Dad said I hadn't either. I always said that Lisa was afraid she was going to miss something, but maybe this was just me remembering how I felt.

Because I was so incredibly hyper, Mommy just couldn't seem to cope with me, especially during her pregnancies. It wasn't that I misbehaved or got into trouble—Dad wouldn't have put up with that. I was just too active for her sensitive demeanor—since I didn't take naps, she couldn't get any rest. And too, she had very difficult pregnancies, compounded by the number of miscarriages she had before I came along. She had horrible bouts of nausea and often felt weak and sick.

Even though the doctors warned her of the danger of bearing more children, Mommy and Dad so desperately wanted a family that she was willing to take the risk. Linda Lou's birth was terribly hard on her, but Dusty's was even worse. On the very day that she and the baby were supposed to come home from the hospital, she suffered a blood clot. Five days after Dusty's birth, Mommy died in November of 1946.

Mommy's death was devastating for us all. Nana had just gotten Linda Lou and me all dressed up to welcome Mommy and our new baby brother. We were so excited and had been looking forward to this for five days. But Mommy didn't come home. First, I remember that Nana started crying—but she wouldn't say why. Soon, my Aunt Neen, Mommy's sister-in-law, came over to be with Nana. I don't remember who told us, but finally someone did. We were told that the baby would not be coming home yet and that Mommy wouldn't be coming at all—she had gone to heaven to be with God.

Now I knew who God was. Linda and I went to Sunday school each and every week and, thanks to Mommy and Nana, I was already winning bookmarks for reciting Bible verses from memory. But, at the age of six, it was just too much for me to grasp that Mommy was with God and couldn't be with us at the same time.

The next two days were horrid and disorienting. We just couldn't understand what was happening and kept asking when

Mommy and the baby were coming home. The house was in chaos. There were Nana and Granddaddy, people from the studio, friends trying to get inside through the gang of reporters waiting outside. It seemed that the phone just wouldn't stop ringing. Believe me, it was a lot more than a six-year-old and a three-year-old could handle.

What is strange is that I don't recall Dad's role in this at all. He was probably with Mommy's brother, Uncle Don, making funeral arrangements.

A couple of days later, which was the day of the funeral, Marian Christiansen, mother of Dad's stand-in Whitey, and her friend, Virginia Peck, showed up to take care of Linda and me. Dad was getting ready to attend Mommy's funeral but Linda Lou and I were told that we couldn't go—this was just for adults. Nana and Granddaddy, Aunt Neen and Uncle Don picked up Dad and left for the funeral. The house suddenly got really quiet for the first time in days. Everyone we knew was gone. Linda and I were alone with two women we had just met, while everyone else was saying goodbye to Mommy. I think that is when I made up my mind to be an adult as soon as possible. I remember being absolutely furious with Dad, Nana, and everyone in sight. I pitched a screaming fit, something I rarely did. I couldn't believe that the adults got to say goodbye to Mommy and we were excluded just because we were little kids. From that time on, my main goal in life was to be an adult and make my own decisions. My husband, Larry, says that he never saw anyone so obsessed with wanting to be a "grown-up," even when we were in high school together. But I really resented being a child and even a teenager. And it all started with the helplessness I felt when my Mommy died.

2

Meet Dale Evans

On the **June 9, 1945,** issue of the *Saturday Evening Post*, there's a feature story on my Dad titled "Cincinnati Cowboy." It's illustrated with color photos of Dad reading to Linda Lou and me, Mommy serving a lemon meringue pie—just like the one she snared Dad with—and, of course, Trigger. On one page is a fascinating—and coincidental—picture spread. At the bottom is a shot of me, Mommy and Dad in front of Dad's pigeon coops; and just above it is a shot of Dad with his current co-star, Miss Dale Evans.

I already knew Dale Evans very well—and I was crazy about her. Many of the studio's leading actresses didn't like having a little kid around since they were so young themselves; most of them were in their late teens or early twenties. Having a little kid around asking a million questions just wasn't cool. But Dale wasn't like that, and I was fascinated by her. More important, she seemed to like me and never talked down to me. She was one star who didn't mind if I got into her makeup. Maybe it was because she was a little older when she came to Hollywood and already had a child of her own, but she was different than the other ladies in Dad's movies, and we were both from Texas!

She was born Frances Octavia Smith on October 31, 1912, at her maternal grandparents' home in Uvalde, Texas. From the beginning, she always wanted to do things her own way. She was extremely precocious and skipped several grades, graduating from high school at 13, which, of course, made her too young to do the things or have the freedom that her classmates did.

Dale was fascinated by music and dancing but she grew up in a Southern Baptist household where music was what you sang in church and dancing was a sin. For such a free spirit, this was an extremely restrictive life.

She eloped with her high school sweetheart and married at 14. It turned out to be a disastrous move. They were two kids playing house; neither of them thought about what would happen if they became a family. As usually happens when the parents are teenagers, he didn't want to be an adult yet. Mom told me that he abandoned her several times. But she still resisted when her parents pressured her to get a divorce. Finally she had no choice but to listen to her parents and by the age of 17 she was a single parent, raising her little boy, Tommy.

While Dad always said that his career was an accident, Mom was truly driven to perform. Tommy says that she sang all the time; in the car, at her desk, even doing dishes. She copyrighted her first song at 16 and soon began performing on radio broadcasts in Tennessee, Kentucky, Illinois, and Texas. More than that, she also married twice more along the way. She sang with big bands in some of the most famous showrooms in Chicago and San Francisco.

While appearing at the Coconut Grove in Los Angeles, she was offered a contract at 20th Century Fox. She signed a two-picture deal with an option. She made the two pictures, *Orchestra Wives* (1942) and *Girl Trouble* (1942), but they didn't pick up her option. As one of the executives told her, they already had a Betty Grable.

The one good thing that happened in Hollywood was that when her first agent was drafted during World War II, she hired Art Rush to be her new manager. Art got her a job on the *Chase & Sanborn Hour*, one of the top radio shows of its day. She was now co-starring with some of the biggest stars of the '40s: Edgar Bergen and Charlie McCarthy; Don Ameche; Jimmy Durante; Garry Moore; and Fran Allison, Mom's good friend who later became the star of TV's *Kukla, Fran and Ollie*. Mom said that they were very generous about sharing their experiences and helping her prepare for her next movie opportunity.

That opportunity came along when she signed with Republic Pictures. Republic was well known for its exciting serials and also for its low-budget but highly popular Westerns. Mom was hoping to be in MGM musicals, but she recognized that Republic would offer her opportunities that she might not get elsewhere. One of the plusses of the studio was that it kept its contract players working all the time—Mom appeared in *five* feature films in 1943 alone! One of them was a John Wayne western, *In Old Oklahoma* (1943; later renamed *War of the Wildcats*), where she got to showcase her singing and dancing talents as she played the lead singer in the chorus. I've always loved her character's name in that film—Cuddles. Most of the other films were light, musical comedies. It seemed that the studio was trying to find a place for her. She showed plenty of versatility, but she was particularly good at playing intelligent, funny, tough women—characters who could give as good as they got.

What she dearly wanted was to be a musical star and if there were some great dramatic roles in the mix, so much the better. What she *didn't* want to be was a Western star, even though she enjoyed making the film with Wayne and was a huge fan of his. She often said that when she first came to Hollywood, the only autograph she wanted was John Wayne's. Then she chickened out and didn't ask him when the opportunity was presented.

But even though she didn't want to appear in Westerns, fate had some surprises in store for her. Herbert Yates had seen Rodgers and Hammerstein's groundbreaking musical *Oklahoma* on Broadway and was really impressed with it. Yates got the idea that he wanted to do something different at Republic—instead of the fast-paced serials and B-Westerns, his studio would produce big-budget Western musicals. And even though "big-budget" at Republic didn't mean quite the same thing that it did at Paramount or Fox, Yates obviously wanted to do something special.

Yates always intended Dad to star in the first of these productions but he didn't have a co-star in mind. They decided that Dale, who was an established radio star, would be the one most likely to fill the role opposite Dad in *The Cowboy and the Señorita* (1944). They knew she could sing and dance. When they asked her if she could ride a horse, she replied, "Well, I *am* from Texas, aren't I?" So naturally, they assumed that she could ride a horse. Mom didn't lie, but like most actresses, she didn't always give an entirely straight answer. Actors never admit they can't do something if they want the part. The simple truth was, she couldn't ride a horse. The only things she had ever ridden were the goats at her uncle's ranch in Texas. She immediately went to the stables at Griffith Park to take riding lessons. She also had a couple of stunt-doubles who were outstanding riders, and they made her look good.

As soon as *The Cowboy and the Señorita* was released and people saw them together, that did it—the studio knew they had found the perfect match for Roy. Every time that Republic would cast another lady opposite Dad they got lots of letters demanding the return of Dale Evans. From the moment they appeared on-screen together, there was magic between them. They had something really extraordinary together. My husband, Larry, always says they proved the whole is greater than the sum of its parts. They both had good, solid individual careers, but together they created an entity that is still known today, more than sixty years later. Around the world, if you say Roy and Dale, everyone over the age of 40—and even some younger folks—will know that you mean Roy Rogers and Dale Evans.

3

Sky Haven Ranch

Right after Mommy died, Dad sold the house on Longridge and bought a ranch above Lake Hughes called Sky Haven Ranch. It was a rustic place set high on a mesa. We lived there with the two women who had been brought in to take care of us kids after Mommy's death: Marian Christensen, who was the widowed mother of Dad's stand-in; and her friend Virginia Peck, who was also widowed.

Sky Haven Ranch was beautiful but really bleak. Like so many hilltops in Southern California, there's not much vegetation because the winds are so awful. Did I say the ranch was rustic? It was almost like a pioneer's cabin. The ranch consisted of a small main house with a bunkhouse over the root cellar. The house was so small that there was only enough room for three people. Mrs. Christiansen, Linda Lou, and Dusty took up residence there while Virginia and I shared the bunkhouse. There was a water pump on the sink and you had to fill a basin and take it in and fill the tank of the toilet. It did have a toilet that flushed; it just didn't have running water. At night, Virginia and I had to use the outhouse because Marian was terrified about living out in the middle of absolutely nowhere and kept the house locked up tight. One morning Virginia came to see what was taking me so long in the outhouse. I told her that I was watching the pretty worms. She opened the door and almost died of fright. My "pretty worms" were newly hatched baby rattlesnakes.

This had once been a working ranch so there was a big barn. It seemed a great distance from the house; I'm sure it probably wasn't, but to a six-year-old it seemed like forever. There was another area down the road that had a small house on it where I the foreman and his family lived.

I remember going to a one-room school house in Lake Hughes. We had to come down off the mesa, driving on a steep winding dirt road to go down to school. The school educated kids from kindergarten through eighth grade. To me it was sort of a continuation of the studio school that I loved so much because we had students of all ages. I was as happy as could be because I never did my *own* school work—I was always working two or three grades ahead because that was far more interesting to me.

Transportation was a real concern. Whenever there were several days of rain or harsh weather of any kind, including the occasional snow storm, we were pretty much trapped up on top of the mesa. To do any shopping or pick up a package or anything like that, we had to drive all the way into Lancaster, which was a far distance from where we were and seemed to take forever to a six-year-old.

Every other week Virginia or Mrs. Christiansen would drive Linda Lou and me down to Nana and Granddaddy Wilkins', so we could spend the weekend with them. Every once in a while, we traveled down to Hollywood to appear in a magazine layout or fulfill some other professional obligation. Those were always nice, because it was one of the few times we'd actually get to see Dad; I really don't remember seeing much of him otherwise during the year we lived there.

The ranch might have seemed a little primitive to some people, but to Dad it was his dream come true. Remember that he grew up in Duck Run, Ohio. Even today Duck Run is a rural community but when Dad was a boy, it was in the middle of nowhere. My grandfather worked away from home and came home only every other weekend. That's how Dad was raised. By the time Dad was seven he was the one who put meat on the table. And that is how he learned his incredible shooting skills. He learned how to trap and he was deadly with a slingshot. When Dad was nine years old, Grampy gave him his first gun. Grampy would leave him with only three or four shells, for two weeks (that was all they could afford). That meant if Dad missed they didn't have meat—a great incentive to become a really good shot, really fast.

Dad thought the ranch was just beautiful. To me, it wasn't beautiful at all—I remember it as being just plain bleak, with a great supply of rattlesnakes and the largest lizards I had ever seen. Somehow, the beauty and ambience were lost on me. But all that mattered to Dad was that he now owned a big ranch. After his hardscrabble childhood, this must have been a really big deal for him. But as much as he loved the place, he never lived there at all. There was no room for him! He stayed at the home of Glenn Randall, his good friend and Trigger's trainer, which was also practically right around the corner from Republic.

But even though he didn't live there with us, Dad had big plans for the place. One day, construction began on a large, two-story house. We thought Dad was just making a better place for us to live. We didn't know that he was also about to make a major change in his life—one that would affect all of our lives forever.

4

A Royal Wedding

s an adult you look back on things and find a far different perspective than what you knew as a child. Today, I think it's pretty clear that there was a strong attraction between Dad and Mom from the very beginning. The chemistry, despite all their differences, probably made their marriage inevitable.

How could anyone resist her? She was beautiful, warm, and funny. How could anyone resist him, his charm and good looks? They really did make a fabulous couple, on- and offscreen.

During the year that we lived at Sky Haven Ranch, Dad's romance with Mom was growing—but we kids didn't have a clue. That beautiful two-story house he was building on the mesa was for her.

Afterwards, Mom always loved to tell everyone "their story."

The autumn following Mommy's death, Dad and Dale were appearing together in a rodeo at Chicago Stadium. Just before they were to ride out on horseback and start their act, Dad asked her what she was doing New Year's Eve.

She was puzzled by the question. It was only the fall of 1947—New Year's Day wasn't for three or four months yet. She told Dad that, as far as she knew, she had no plans and asked him why he wanted to know.

Dad grinned and said, "Well then, why don't we get married?" just as the announcer shouted, "Ladies and Gentlemen—Roy

Rogers!" Trigger reared, then he and Dad burst out of the chute to wild applause from the huge crowd. As he made the circle of the arena, she thought about taking on three motherless children. She later said that for a moment she wasn't sure that she could do it, but she had always wanted a big family and she felt sorry for us kids . . . of course, she was wild about Dad too. . .

Then the words, ". . . and Miss Dale Evans!"

Mom rode out on horseback and took her place at Dad's side, acknowledging the cheers of the audience. Dad glanced over at her expectantly and Mom mouthed the word, "Yes!" Then, together, they finished the rest of their act.

When they were out of the arena, he leaned toward her and stretched out his hand. In his hand was a box. Inside the box was a gold ring, adorned with a beautiful ruby, which he slipped on Mom's finger. Now, how many people have *that* kind of engagement story?

That's when, with their marriage approaching, Dad unveiled his special surprise. He brought her up to Sky Haven Ranch and showed her the house he was building. In their dual autobiography, *Happy Trails,* Mom described her first visit to Sky Haven this way:

"It wasn't anything grand—just a little house surrounded by flowering almond trees, alongside a smooth lake where ducks paddled around. I watched his daughters, Cheryl and Linda, greet him with big hugs; and I saw the joy in the face of baby Dusty (Roy Jr.) when his daddy bent down to hold him. The happiness they shared was so plain, I ached. And strangely—wonderfully—I felt completely at home. I *was* home."

Well, that's a lovely description—but not precisely how things really went. My memory is a bit different. Mom took one look at the house under construction and said there was no way she was going to live out there in the middle of nowhere! I think my memory might be a little better than hers because of the events that followed. I can't remember her ever spending a night in that house. She also said, upon learning of the one-room schoolhouse, that Linda and I needed to have a proper education—and that meant living in town!

Dad was disappointed, but to this day I don't know what he was thinking about, trying to get to her live at Sky Haven. They needed *her* paycheck as much as they needed his. In fact, at the time, she was making as much as he was. Originally, in 1943 when she was hired by Republic, she made a better salary there than Dad or even John Wayne! There was no way she could live that far away from the studio, which was about a two-hour drive in those days.

Anyway, she and Dad were making their plans, and Linda Lou and I still knew nothing about what the adults around us were doing.

Mom and Dad got married on New Year's Eve of 1947, during a blizzard, at a friend's ranch in Oklahoma. Dad—Mister Romance!—took his new bride coon hunting the next day. Poor Mom! But she was nothing if not a good sport. When they returned to California, they found a home in the Hollywood Hills that had formerly belonged to Noah Beery Jr. It was on a hillside overlooking the city, had terraced grounds, and was large enough for a big family.

Their marriage led to some professional troubles for Mom. The studio was not at all pleased about their wedding. The publicity department had been playing up the "widower/eligible bachelor" bit to the hilt with Dad

Mom had given the story of the wedding to columnist Hedda Hopper, who broke it in her column the next day as an "exclusive." Hedda's main competition, Louella Parsons, was furious. She wrote horrible things about Mom and Dad in her column because she hadn't gotten the exclusive. Today it's hard for people to understand how powerful these two ladies were—but they wielded huge influence in Hollywood, and celebrities lived or died by what was in their columns.

Louella had always loved Dad, and she had liked Mom. But when Hedda's story broke, Louella wrote a horrible story about Mom passing Tommy off as her brother when in reality he was her son. Louella indicated in the article that Mom had done it because Mom was somehow perpetrating a fraud on Hollywood. Of course, at that time, movie actresses were all supposed to be twenty, unmarried and childless. Mom's former agent had insisted that Mom keep her age a secret so, of course, she couldn't have a teenage son when she was supposed to be 25.

It was a mean and spiteful story. But I think Mom and Dad were most upset because it might cause Tommy to be hurt. I've never discussed this with him, but I hope that he and his wife, Barbara, were too happy and too much in love themselves to have paid attention to a bitter lady trying to hurt him to get "even" with Mom and Dad over a perceived slight to her Hollywood position.

Mr. Yates, head of Republic, was reported to be so incensed by the marriage that he actually suspended Mom from Dad's pictures. For a while, it looked as if she might have to live at Sky Haven Ranch after all!

But the wedding created more of a stir closer to home—with me. I was even more furious about their marriage than Republic was. Even though I had adored Dale for years, I now saw her as an intruder into our family. When Mommy died, Dad told me that I was the big sister and that it was my job to take care of Linda Lou and my baby brother Dusty—I was in charge. Well, I thought being in charge was really cool, if not, in fact, my birthright—after all, I was the oldest! I took my responsibilities very seriously.

I don't know if it would have made any difference whether or not Dad shared his excitement and optimism with us before they got married. Unfortunately, Dad rarely let us in on any of his plans. He almost always kept his own counsel, even with Mom. Just as Sky Haven had come as a complete surprise and not a little bit of a shock to her, the marriage was a complete shock to me.

I now wonder if Dad didn't simply assume that since his kids needed a Mom, since Linda and I adored Dale, and since he was happy, we would be delighted to have her as our new mother. But, while Dale had always been my hero, when she and Dad got married, all of a sudden *she* was the woman in charge, a usurper, and my rival. That was a really big deal and I didn't like it *at all*!

5

School Days

I was so upset at their marriage that I refused to live with them. It had been difficult coping with losing Mommy, but then Dad moved us to the back of beyond, away from him, away from all of our friends and everyone familiar. Now, just a short year later, we were moving again, this time to Hollywood, to another new house, new school, new everything. It just seemed like too many changes for a kid to make.

Shortly after the wedding, Mom was showing Linda Lou and me pictures taken at the wedding. Mom's parents were there. Lots of their friends were there. And, there were Mom's son, Tom, and his fiancée, Barbara. To a child who hated missing any party, I took this as an almost personal insult and viewed it as one more example of how kids were always excluded from important events. This further strengthened my resolve to grow up as soon as I could.

Feeling shoved out of my job and position in the family, I was most unhappy and, I'm now embarrassed to say, I made sure that everybody around me was unhappy, too. I told them I didn't want to live with them, that I would rather go away and live somewhere else. I don't know where I had heard about boarding school at that age, but I insisted that was the only thing that would make me happy.

Even though I was only seven years old, they took my feelings seriously and enrolled me at Villa Cabrini, a Catholic convent and boarding school, at the foot of the mountains in Glendale.

To this day, I'm not quite sure why Mom and Dad allowed me—at seven—to engineer a decision like that. I am sure Mom's feelings were really hurt by my behavior; she and I had always been such close friends. I had always adored her, so my anger toward her was probably a big surprise. Knowing Dad, I doubt very much that he had told her that he was saving her introduction into our household as a secret. I'm sure that anytime the subject of us kids arose, he had assured her that we would be delighted with their secret and would welcome our new "Mom" with open arms!

Or, maybe they thought we might be so excited about the wedding that we wouldn't be able to keep it a secret and the news would get out before they were married?

Even though I know Mom was terribly hurt and puzzled by my behavior (she told me this often in the years following), she was still a good sport and was willing to try anything to achieve détente.

Villa Cabrini was great. Its students ranged from kindergarten through the second year of college. As usual, I would make friends with the girls three or four years ahead of me in school. Villa Cabrini was a Catholic school—we weren't Catholic, by the way—and was known for its scholastic excellence. I had always loved school and managed to make good grades, even with all the moving about. I was lucky that I had sat in on all of those studio classes and had been in a one-room schoolhouse and had Nana and Mommy as my first teachers. These had all given me a good start, and I found the schoolwork to be pretty easy, which I soon learned is not the general perception of Catholic school. Of course, I was only in second grade and the nuns were only too happy to assign extra credit work that would keep me busy. It's too bad that this wasn't always the case. In fact, when attending public schools, it was usually so easy for me that I was often a little bored. I sometimes thought it was so easy, that it was just a waste of my time—which further fueled my desire to get out of school and into the adult world.

I was at Villa Cabrini for just over a year, from spring 1948 to spring 1949. Although I had a good time there and enjoyed the classes, I really missed Linda Lou. But the big gap in my life was not going to the studio with Dad. For the first time in my life, I was separated from that magical place where all my troubles disappeared.

It was during this time that the polio scare swept the country and the entire school was quarantined. That meant if you went home, you couldn't come back to school. There were two or three very lonely months without any visits from family or even grandparents, and without being able to leave campus.

Although I enjoyed the classes and the camaraderie at Villa Cabrini, I can't say the same about the cuisine. This school served us food that can only be described one way—inedible! I swear, there was not a nun at that convent who could cook. The only decent food we ever had was on Parents' Visiting Day, which fell on Sundays. That's when the "cooks" would heat up canned Chef Boyardee spaghetti. Believe me, it was the only decent meal of the whole week! The food was so bad, in fact, that I developed a penchant for pouring tons of pepper and ketchup on everything, just to give it some taste.

As weird as it seems, the horrible food turned out to be kind of a blessing in disguise. During the spring semester of 1949, I got very ill—fever, vomiting—a result, no doubt, of that awful cooking. So ill that the school officials and doctors believed I was coming down with polio. They immediately called Mom and Dad to come get me. I not only got to go home to recuperate but because of the quarantine, I wouldn't be allowed to return.

By this time, my anger over the marriage had subsided a bit. I had made a friend, Judy Kelly, in our new neighborhood over the previous summer, and I really missed Linda Lou and even Dusty. Consequently, I was finally willing to "compromise" and live at home with my family.

It wasn't long before my relationship with Mom improved dramatically. And it was helped along by a little stranger. An angel was about to join our family.

6

Robin, Our Angel

The **year before Mom died,** during the holidays, she was really sick. We didn't think she was going to make it and I *know* the doctors didn't think she was going to make it. The doctors thought she was very depressed. Well, of course she was depressed! She had lost Dad, she was sick and in the hospital, she wasn't spending the holidays with her family, she had a bad heart. Who wouldn't be depressed? I was deeply concerned about her, but I did not see any evidence that she was ready to go—Mom was too much of a fighter. I visited her every day and on one occasion, she seemed especially down. The doctors had given her some drugs that made her a little groggy, but more than that, she seemed very concerned with something. As I sat by her bedside, I asked her what was going on.

Mom looked at me sadly and said, "I wish I had been able to accomplish more in my lifetime."

I must have looked at her as though she were crazy. "What in heaven's name are you talking about?" I said. "You changed the world! Who gets to do that?"

Mom wrote twenty-nine books over the course of her life. Each one, in its way, had a great impact on its readers. But one of them, *Angel Unaware*, literally changed the way that handicapped children and adults are looked at and treated. It was the story of the very brief life of my sister Robin, born with Down syndrome. It was also the story of the impact she had on our lives; and Mom's book had a powerful impact on millions of others' lives.

But Robin's story must begin with the story of my mother's deep Christian faith.

Shortly after Mom married Dad, our new big brother, Tom Fox, married his fiancée, Barbara. Linda Lou and I even got to be flower girls. I had always wanted a big brother, and I almost forgave Mom for marrying Dad when I found out that Tommy came with the package. Mom felt that her new family should have the same religious foundation that she enjoyed as a child. Linda and I went to the Methodist Church in Van Nuys every weekend we spent at Nana's. But Mom said that after three failed marriages, she felt that only God could help her have the happy family she craved.

Tom and Barbara were very strong Christians. They attended Fountain Avenue Baptist Church in Hollywood and invited Mom and their new family to join them. Within a couple of weeks, Mom had rededicated her life to Jesus. Dad resisted for a bit but he and I, seeing how happy and at peace Mom was, were baptized together a few months later. Mom has said in many of her books that if she had not rejoined the Church prior to Robin's birth, she never would have had the moral or mental strength to withstand the incredible pressures of dealing with what was to come.

When Mom and Dad told Linda, Dusty, and me that they were expecting a baby, the last wall between Mom and me came tumbling down. I was ten and couldn't think of anything more wonderful than to have a little brother or sister that I could mother. I could show Mom that I deserved responsibility and, more important, I'd have a "living, breathing doll" to play with and help raise. Dusty, however, wasn't so thrilled. He said that he would *much* rather have a puppy. But, in our family, things seldom worked out the way we expected them to.

Our family finances were predicated on two incomes. For this reason, Mom said that she worked at the beginning of her pregnancy because she knew that the moment she started showing, she wouldn't be able to work again until after the baby's birth. Even though she was experiencing all-day sickness instead of morning sickness, she kept working. At that time, films were shot on a six-day workweek and Mom and Dad were also doing a weekly radio show.

Mom was 38 years old when she became pregnant. Today this would be considered a high-risk pregnancy but, with so many women opting for careers as young women and motherhood later in life, it's not rare at all. In 1950, it was unusual. Linda and I didn't have any friends with mothers Mom's age who were adding to their families.

Her work schedule during this time was frantic: up at 5:00, in hair and makeup before seven. Film scenes and, in between, read the script and work on music for the radio program. They were still doing musical numbers so there might be dance numbers to rehearse or, since they made Westerns, she might be doing scenes on horseback. Return home around 8:00, eat, rehearse the next day's lines, collapse into bed around 10:00. Then do it again the next day. And, at the same time, be a mom to three stepchildren between the ages of ten and three.

She had the usual complications of a normal pregnancy but at some point early on, she was exposed to and caught German measles. Mom also fell down the flight of stairs connecting the bedrooms to the living room. While it had started as a normal pregnancy, this was turning out to be a very difficult one. She and Dad also had to deal with potential problems of her blood being Rh-negative and his Rh-positive—the classic Rh factor conflict. The doctors were concerned that the baby might need a transfusion immediately following its birth.

Robin Elizabeth Rogers was delivered August 2, 1950. Mom said that even though she was ecstatic to have a daughter, she had an overriding sense that something was seriously wrong—the doctors and nurses had long faces, everyone was very solicitous, and Dad was very subdued. Every time she would ask to see the baby, an excuse would be given as to why she couldn't see her at the moment: she was being changed, she was sleeping, or they were doing tests.

Finally, her doctor told her that Robin was very fragile. She had been born with Down syndrome and suffered most of the attendant problems associated with that malady: a weak heart with a leaky valve, trouble eating, and so on. At that time, Down syndrome was practically a death sentence—most doctors just gave up hope as soon as they saw the child. Mom and Dad's doctors actually advised them not to bring Robin home from the hospital. "You don't want to get too attached," they said. "It will only break your heart. This baby will never have a normal life, she will never live past two years of age, she will never be able to read or do anything else."

"Besides," the doctors said, "the baby won't know the difference anyway. She won't even remember you from one visit to another."

Mom and Dad didn't listen to those doctors. Robin was their child and she was going to be raised as part of the family. Before they brought Robin home, they talked to us kids and told us that our new sister was very sick and very delicate and we were going to have to be quiet and considerate of her needs. They asked us if we thought we could do it. We promised that we would rise to the challenge—and that's quite a feat for a boisterous family like ours.

Mom always credited Dad with being the first to say that Robin was coming to live with us. She said that he figured God had a purpose for placing Robin in our lives and in our family, and that it wasn't up to us to question what God had in mind. They made arrangements to provide twenty-four-hour care for Robin and as soon as she had gained enough weight and was in stable health, Robin joined our family.

One of the first little miracles that Robin performed was to bring my mother and me closer together. We had gotten friendlier in the time since I returned from Villa Cabrini. Then Mom endured this horrible pregnancy. By that time I was ten years old and *very* female. She was carrying our new baby and she was suffering so, that I became very supportive. During her pregnancy, then the heartbreaking days after Robin's birth, we became closer than ever. Sick children can sometimes tear families apart, but in our case it brought us closer together. Robin changed our world without ever knowing it.

Robin was, of course, very fragile, but she was a full-fledged member of the Rogers family from the moment we met her. In those days, Down syndrome kids were kept out of sight, as if their condition were shameful or an embarrassment of some sort. But Robin was always front and center in our lives. When photographers came to our house to shoot layouts, Robin was always a part of it. Mom and Dad never tried to hide her. Sometimes, they had to protect her from getting too excited, but other than that they were right up front. They declared that God gave her to them for a purpose and she wasn't going to be hidden in a back room.

I didn't realize at the time how courageous they were in taking this stand—the studio was very upset with them. To the public relations department, a child with Down syndrome was the ultimate in bad publicity. They were convinced that Mom and Dad would repel their fans by "flaunting" this sick child. Even the people at church disapproved. Some of them believed—and even said aloud—that a child with a handicap was a punishment, that the parent had clearly committed some terrible sin and this child was the result.

The house in the Hollywood Hills was literally built into the hillside of Iverine Street. It was three stories high and you had to go up and down stairs constantly. Dad and Mom soon decided that we needed a home that would have space for everyone and that would provide Robin with the peace and security she needed. Dad found us the perfect home in Encino. The property consisted of seven acres, so Dad could finally have his farm. There was a main house, two small pool houses, a pool, a tennis court, and enough room to keep our own milk cow. But we had to buy goats' milk for Robin. We could grow most of our own vegetables, and raise most of our own meat. There was also plenty of room to build a two-room cottage for Robin and her nurse, away from all of her boisterous siblings.

Robin may have been sickly, but she was a loving baby. She enjoyed being in the house and in the middle of things. We were used to going in and out every day to see her and play with her. She knew all of us and as she started learning to talk she gave us all nicknames. She also loved to stand up and could with only a little help. But about the time for her to start crawling and walking, she stopped making progress. Because Down syndrome doesn't normally cause problems like that, my concerned parents took Robin back to the hospital. After a thorough checkup, the doctors made an astonishing and heartbreaking discovery— Robin had contracted polio. There didn't seem to be an end to what this little girl was being forced to endure.

Robin was soon fitted for a brace to help straighten her legs. Now her days had a new activity—physical therapy. How she survived any of this is completely beyond me—a weak heart and immune system, and the hole in her heart that never fully closed, how much could one baby take?

Even so, she was a beautiful and sunny little girl who loved everyone, typical of children with Down's. Any day that she was well enough to come into the house and eat with us, or that we could spend time playing with her, was a wonderful day. When she was ailing, we all felt terrible. What a short life of terrible challenges and pain, and what a sweet baby she was through it all. I think the fact that she faced all of this with such good cheer gave us hope that she really would be victorious in the end, that she would somehow conquer her frailties and get well. That's why every day that she was with us, hope grew that she would live to that magic fifth birthday. But then came a challenge that proved too much for her and we lost her.

About three days before she died, the doctors told Mom and Dad that Robin could not survive for much longer. She had contracted mumps which had in turn developed into brain fever— encephalitis. While you can never be prepared to lose a child, no matter what the circumstances, we knew the time had finally come and we had to accept it.

During this period, Mom occupied herself by holding Robin, praying for a miracle and instructing us in our responsibilities for when the actual moment arrived. She believed, as I do, that if you had a job to do, you could better deal with tragedy.

Virginia Peck, who was now our housekeeper, would prepare for those who would be arriving for the services. Emily Warren, our cook, would begin preparing food for the family and friends who would be there. And I was assigned the job of calling the people on Mom's list of those to be notified.

Robin died early on the morning two days prior to her second birthday. While Mom and Dad consoled each other, the rest of us went about our assigned tasks. I called our minister, Father Harley Wright Smith, first. He had been waiting for the call and came over immediately. Then I called their manager, Art Rush. One of his tasks was to notify the media, and he already had a press release prepared. The news broke almost immediately on the local radio stations. Anything to do with the Roy Rogers family was big news, especially the death of a child.

The house had been almost silent for the days preceding Robin's death; everyone talked in whispers and tiptoed around. Now it was swarming with people. Thanks to Art's preparations and quick action, although there were a couple of photographers outside the gates, none of them were calling the house or trying to come onto our property. I was still busy notifying people on Mom's list.

The next few days were total chaos. Thanks to Art's adroit handling, the media were being good. He was giving them enough information that they weren't bothering Mom and Dad. But it was hard to get in or out of our driveway because of people parked on either side of the street, waiting to get a glimpse of the family.

Some people wanted more than a glimpse. The day Robin died, a car pulled into our yard bearing Minnesota plates. Inside were two women and four or five children. Dad stepped outside to meet them.

"Oh, Mr. Rogers," one of them said, "This is such a thrill to meet you. All of us are such big fans and since we were so close, we thought it would be so wonderful to see where you live."

My father was always very kind to his fans so he said gently, "I'm sorry, this isn't a good time. My daughter has just passed away."

"Oh yes," the woman said brightly. "We heard about it on the radio. We're so very sorry. But we have to go home from our vacation tomorrow, so we knew it was now or never!"

I've seen my father angry before, but never that angry. He told those women in no uncertain terms that they were to turn that car around and take it back to wherever they came from. And he added a few choice words about their characters in general.

The women were completely shocked and indignant at Dad's outburst. Didn't he realize that they had driven out all this way to see him and his family and tour their property? Is this the way he treated his fans?

Dad said, with barely controlled fury, "Get off my land. Now!"

They reluctantly left and, no doubt, spent the rest of their lives telling people that Roy Rogers wasn't nearly as sweet in person as he appeared to be in the movies. I thought Dad was going to rip their heads off, and I don't think I would have blamed him if he had.

(Under most circumstances Dad was invariably polite to people, whatever the provocation, because being an actor there were always guys in a restaurant or something saying things like, "Oh, I saw you in a fight in that movie and you aren't so tough!" Even though Dad didn't provoke that type of aggressive behavior as much as a lot of the others—he was such a nice guy—he still got some of it. That's the part of fame that has always disturbed and confused me; I can never understand how people think that they can intrude on some-one's privacy like that. But of all the inappropriate people, those two women who came to our house the day Robin died, well, they take the cake.)

Mom and Dad were devastated by the loss of Robin; we all were. They had a show to do at Madison Square Garden in New York and Mom always said that was the luckiest thing for her, be-cause it was a commitment they couldn't get out of and it helped to keep their minds off their grief. While there, she started think-ing about putting some of her thoughts about Robin down on paper. She met with her friend Dr. Norman Vincent Peale and told him what she was thinking about doing. He advised her that writ-ing a book could be good therapy.

Dr. Peale may have advised Mom to write the book, but she al-ways said that the book itself was given to her by God. Maybe that's true, because the book just poured out of her—it took her no time at all to complete. She told me that it was something He wanted said at that time—and all she had to do was write it down! I thought, and still think, that it's wonderful that she could take something that difficult, that hard to deal with, that tragic and turn it into something positive that not only helped her and our family, but millions of other people, all over the world.

She wrote *Angel Unaware* mostly for her own peace of mind but the book was an immediate sensation. It stayed on the *New York Times* bestseller list for more than four months. *Angel Unaware* has, to date, been through nearly thirty printings, in several languages and in both hardcover and paperback. It has been read by untold millions of people around the world—and Mom never made a penny from it. She gave every cent she earned from it to the National Association for Retarded Children, which was still a relatively young, struggling organization. There was not a great deal of research being done because the money simply wasn't there to fund it; the organization was little more than a group of concerned parents and doctors who were trying to do *something*.

Mom's little book gave them the money to start the research and form a real association: The Arc of the United States (now known just as The Arc). Even today, I get statements from the organization stating that the book has brought them $7,000 or $12,000 that year—and that's fifty years after *Angel Unaware* was first published!

But we saw the benefits of the book in other ways, too. When we would go out on tour, doing personal appearances at state fairs and rodeos or other big events, it was always our practice to go to that particular city's local children's hospital or the children's ward of a general hospital. We would do a show for the kids, then Dad and Mom would talk with them individually and maybe sign autographs. But we never saw kids with Down syndrome or other forms of retardation. And kids like that *certainly* didn't attend the rodeo or the state fair or any of the other places where we performed.

All that started changing within just a couple of years of the publication of *Angel Unaware*. By the time I was about fourteen, we'd be doing a show and there would be a whole group of kids with Down's at the rodeo, right up front. It was incredible to see these kids who had been hidden away, finally allowed to lead happy and fulfilling lives, having fun and being thrilled by the sights and sounds of a rodeo, just like "normal" kids.

My husband, Larry, has a cousin named Terry who was born with Down syndrome, the very late/change-of-life child of older parents. Terry's about fifty now. His parents have been gone for a very long time and Terry lives happily in a sheltered group home where he works and supports himself. He's a really dear and funny guy, always telling jokes, always proud of his accomplishments. The difference between his life today and what it would have been before *Angel Unaware* is phenomenal. He has mental and physical problems and he doesn't live a "normal" life—but he lives a life in which he finds happiness, fulfillment, companionship, and security, and that's something that couldn't have been conceived of only a few generations ago.

I know that Mom loved the television show *Life Goes On* that starred the young actor Chris Burke, who was born with Down syndrome. She never missed the program and would always talk about what an outstanding young actor he was. Oh, how she wished that Robin could have lived long enough to have benefited from today's medicine, and how society has changed for the better.

And that change has come about, in a very direct way because of the way Mom and Dad lived their lives with Robin, and especially because of *Angel Unaware*. All the ignorance and fear haven't completely disappeared from the world, of course, but the improvement has been incredible. Today, my kids can't even imagine that kind of "dark ages" attitude, thank God. In the world into which Robin was born, Down syndrome kids were something to be ashamed of and hidden away. It's a different world now, thanks, in great part, to my Mom.

As the education director for the museum, I get letters from teachers all the time, especially fourth-grade teachers from all over the country, who use *Angel Unaware* to teach their students tolerance. It speaks to them on a level they can understand immediately. *Angel Unaware* is a great little book. I have to agree with

Mom—I think God gave it to her. But it's very definitely her voice, her accomplishment, her point of view.

Mom was such a gifted woman. She was a good dancer, a great singer, a terrific actress, and a wonderful songwriter. She could come up with script ideas—she even helped Dad rewrite the scripts on their radio and television shows. She was a fine musician. She was a great Mom. Aside from all of those things, what she did for people with Down syndrome, through her writing of *Angel Unaware*, was a sea change. That's why, when she said to me from that hospital bed, that she didn't think she'd accomplished enough in her life, and that there was so much more she still wanted to do, I just couldn't believe my ears. She accomplished more than most people. And in the genuine good that she did—through her talent as well as the books she wrote—she had a powerful and continuing impact.

Not bad for one lifetime, huh?

Our Grandparents

Grandparents can be a very important part of a child's life. I always thought that we were extremely lucky: we had six grandparents. Although they were all very different, we loved visiting and spending time with them. I think it kept us all well-grounded, being part of such diverse families.

Linda Lou and I thought Nana Wilkins was fantastic—the perfect grandmother, just like you read about in books. Nana made cookies and tapioca pudding; she was a great cook. She taught us to embroider, knit, and crochet. She even gave us our first piano lessons. She and Granddaddy took us to the Ice Capades and the movies. She did all of the things Nanas are supposed to do. So I really appreciate the times we had with her. She was always the first person to show up with a casserole or cake if any of her neighbors had a problem and the people who lived on Matilija Street were blessed to have her as a neighbor. Today, I don't have time to do those things with my grandkids and really regret that I can't pass on to my grandkids what my grandparents passed on to me

The only trouble with Nana, was that she was so starstruck. If she had somehow managed to get Mommy to Hollywood as a young girl, Nana would have been the typical stage mother, pushing Mommy and probably making her life miserable.

Just after Mommy (Arline) died, it looked like my grandmother—Nana—was going to take care of us. She sure wanted to—but Dad thought that would be a really bad idea. Nana was a very determined and very outspoken lady—and that's putting it mildly! Nana had pretty much controlled Mommy's life and she wanted to extend that control over us after Mommy's death. Later on, she was very much against Dad remarrying and I remember that she was *completely* against Mom (Dale) and Dad adopting any more brothers and sisters for Linda Lou, Dusty, and me. It was all right that *I* was adopted because I was there before her grand-children came so I was a "real" grandchild. But adopting the rest of the kids—my grandmother had a fit every time, just an absolute fit.

But Mom never lost patience with her. She realized that Nana had lost her only daughter, and Mom felt empathy for every-body. Mom always allowed us to go visit Nana; in fact she en-couraged it. Linda Lou and I spent every other weekend at Nana's house, almost until I was grown. Even when I was in high school I was still going to my Nana's house on a regular basis, but by then it was at Mom's insistence. By that time I was dating and boys were more important than my grandmother, but I was still there a lot.

Nana (Lucille) Wilkins was a Methodist minister's daughter and had very liberal ideas. Grandma Betty Sue Smith, on the other hand, was a Texas rancher's daughter who had been raised a South-ern Baptist. Nana was fascinated with show business and I believe that had she been born today, she would have sought a career in the performing arts. Grandma Smith, on the other hand, thought that music and singing should only be done in church and that dancing was something the devil tempted young people with.

Nana read every movie magazine, "true romance," and "true crime" magazine published. I loved spending the night at her house because she kept the magazines under the bed in the guest-room and I would read them late into the night. Nana demanded to participate in every party Mommy and Dad would give for their Hollywood acquaintances. But I don't think that Grandma Smith ever got really comfortable around Mom's in-volvement with "show people." She was always gracious and warm, for she was, after all, a Southern lady.

Betty Sue was a college graduate who ran the farms that she and Grandfather Hillman Smith owned. Even though she was a very conservative Christian lady, she divorced Grandfather Smith because he was a gambler. They were separated for several years before they reconciled and remarried. From conversations that Mom and I had about that time, I think those years were almost as hard on Mom as they were on Grandma—Mom really adored her Southern aristocrat father. When they remarried, it was with the proviso that Grandfather Smith never have a checkbook and, according to Mom, Grandma kept him on a strict allowance from then on.

From what Mom said, Grandma ran everything in the Smith family; she was a very strong and bright lady. Mom always gave credit to Grandma, publicly and privately, for how Mom and Tommy turned out—she knew that it was Grandma's Christian beliefs and her steadfastness of character that had shown them the way to live their lives.

Granddaddy Prentice Davidson Wilkins came from a background similar to Grandfather Smith. They had both been raised as Southern gentlemen. Where Grandfather Smith moved to Texas as an adult, Granddaddy Wilkins moved from Texas to New Mexico. He opened a hardware store there and was a very popular local politician. When he and Nana moved to Van Nuys, he raised elm trees, camellias, and roses, which he sold wholesale to nurseries in the Valley. I was always fascinated when, each spring, he would take what looked to me like dead twigs, put something that looked like salve on one end, stick the twig in soil, and a few weeks later, a tree would start to grow. I believed that he created miracles.

Granddaddy and Grampy Slye both raised chickens and since I was the oldest, one of my jobs was to collect the fresh eggs. I was proud of being given such an important job, but I was terrified of the roosters guarding the henhouses, with good cause.

Granddaddy and Grandfather Smith were both tall and slender Texans, and they both had wonderful full heads of beautiful white wavy hair. When we were little, Granddaddy Wilkins used to let Linda Lou and me place curlers in his hair, even though they certainly weren't needed; then we would brush it and comb it for what seemed like hours.

Dad's mother, Mattie Slye, was an adorable, tiny person who had been crippled since she was a baby. I never knew for sure why she was crippled. I heard various stories that she contracted polio or that she was injured when she was dropped by an older sister. She had been raised in the hill country of Kentucky and, when *The Beverly Hillbillies* came on TV, I thought that our "Mammy" Slye must have been the inspiration for "Granny"—she was a little, feisty country woman with a very colorful way of speaking. And she wielded incredible authority. She was the one adult who, when she said, "Come here, you little dickens," even my boy cousins, who were really ornery and rotten and in trouble all the time, would go to her sheepishly. She'd tweak our ears and tell us that if we didn't behave she was going to pinch our ears off.

Mammy and Grampy Andrew Slye (Andy) were not well educated. Grampy worked in factories most of his life. He could build almost anything given some lumber, nails, and a little baling wire. He and Dad built the place in Duck Run when Dad was only seven, so you know Grampy did most of the work. But he had to have done a pretty good job because the house is still there.

When Dad began starring in movies, he bought Grampy and Mammy a little farm on Havenhurst by Van Nuys Airport. Grampy raised chickens and Concord grapes from then on. Mammy, like the other grandmothers, was a wonderful cook. Her fried chicken was always fought over at family gatherings but her chicken and flat-rolled German dumplings were so heavy that they would stay with you for days—naturally, that was one of Dad's favorite dishes.

When the grandparents were around, Dad was Leonard and Mom was Francis.

It always tickled us kids to hear Mammy Slye hollering at the TV, "Look out, Leonard, there's a no-good skunk hiding behind that rock!" Or, "Don't you hurt my boy, you varmint, I'll pinch your head off!"

We didn't get to spend much time with the Smith grandparents until after Mom and Dad moved to Apple Valley and Grandma

Smith joined them. Grandfather had passed away some years before and Grandma had finally stopped running the farms in Texas.

Today, I don't have time to do things with my grandkids. I didn't
realize how wonderful it was that the Slyes and Wilkins were
mostly retired when we were kids. Or at least, they worked out of
their homes and were able to give us their love and attention. I regret that I can't give my grandkids what my grandparents gave
me—time.

8

The Rogers Kids

I was the first child my father adopted, but I certainly was not the last. Not by a long shot. In addition to their own kids, Tom, Linda Lou, Dusty and Robin, Mom and Dad adopted three more: John David (Sandy), Mary Doe (Dodie) and Debbie.

My sister Mimi was a British citizen and couldn't be legally adopted by our family, but Mom and Dad sure tried. Whether or not she "officially" had the Rogers surname, it never made any difference to us—she's still our sister.

Our family was eventually made up of many different nationalities, age groups, and personalities. We became our own mini-United Nations.

At first, there was just Linda Lou and me. Almost from the beginning though, we were apart as much as we were together. Because of Mommy's health problems, Linda Lou seemed to spend most of her time with Nana, while I accompanied Dad to the studio. Then we were separated because I was in school and she was home, then I was in private school while she attended classes in public school. The only two times we were even at the same school were at Cheremoya Elementary (in Hollywood) and Encino Elementary. Three years apart in age doesn't sound like much, but it really made a difference.

Linda Lou has always had a beautiful singing voice. In fact, she inherited all of Mommy's artistic and creative abilities and Dad's

musical talent—as has Dusty. Linda knits and crochets beautifully; Dusty builds beautiful homes. When Linda Lou was a
teenager, she could do wonderful impersonations of comedian
Martha Raye and later Carol Burnett. Like Dad, she was a natural
clown and we thought she should go into show business.

Of course, we fought like sisters do. When we lived in Encino,
Linda Lou and I would settle our differences by building a barri-
cade across the doorway separating our bedrooms—we inherited
Robin's two-room cottage—and launching our shoes like missiles
at each other. It was during these conflicts that she would yell out
that I was not really Dad's, I was just adopted. And I would reply,
"They chose me, but they were *stuck* with you!"

Kids have a different concept of fighting fair, especially where
words are concerned. Linda and I had lots of fights over the years
but they weren't serious nor were they different from what other
sisters typically experience, at least I don't think so. Most, if not
all, of our fights ended up with the two of us convulsed by giggles.

Mom always said that one of the reasons she accepted Dad's
marriage proposal was that he promised her she could have a big
family. That was a promise he kept.

Mom was visiting her parents outside of Dallas the April before
Robin died. She went to Hope Cottage to make some inquiries for
me regarding my birth mother. Of course, she always loved to visit
the babies whenever she was there. One of the babies she met was
a four-week-old beauty named Dodie. The baby was a Choctaw
Indian, the same as Dad, and she won Mom's heart with her beautiful dark eyes and serious demeanor. The staff at Hope Cottage
was actively trying to find an Indian family who would adopt her.

I visited family friends in Dallas over the Fourth of July weekend. Mom had previously arranged for me to visit Hope Cottage
and asked me to see if that adorable Indian baby was still there.
Well, she was, and I fell for her too.

When Robin died in August, Mom and Dad were already
scheduled to be in New York in September for a week of performances at Madison Square Garden. Mom often said that the trip
and the work helped to save her sanity. The old show biz tradition
of "the show must go on" can sometimes be a blessing.

Getting ready for the trip, Mom kept thinking about the Indian baby. She called Hope Cottage to see if she was still there. Although they usually kept babies only a short time, they told Mom that, yes, the baby was still there because they hadn't yet found an Indian family to adopt her. They told her there was another interested family but they had no Indian ancestry. Mom begged them to let her have the baby. She told them how much she needed Dodie and, besides, Dad was part Choctaw. They called several times while they were in New York. Just as they were leaving for home, they finally got an answer from Hope Cottage—"Yes!" Mom was so excited.

Mom and Dad sponsored a safety program for elementary schools across the nation. They were scheduled to make a stop in Frankfurt, Kentucky, to present a national safety award to an elementary school there. As usual, while they were in town, they entertained at the local children's home for handicapped kids. That's where they met Sandy.

Mom was worried—Mom was always worried about something—because Dusty was the only boy with two older sisters, and here they were adopting *another* sister. Mom and Dad asked if Sandy was available for adoption. Finding out that Kentucky would be happy to have them take Sandy, they made a quick decision and we got a telegram from Dad saying, "Mom and I will be home Sunday and we are bringing you a surprise."

It didn't seem like much of a surprise to *me*. I knew how much Mom wanted the Indian baby and figured they were bringing her home with them. But it turned out to be a *big* surprise. When they got off the plane, there was our new baby sister and a four-year-old brother John David, who we called Sandy.

He was close to the same age as Dusty but he was the tiniest little guy. Sandy had been abandoned at a motor court when only six weeks old. He had been alone in the bungalow of the court for three or four days before anyone thought to clean the place or check on the crying baby. As a consequence, he suffered from malnutrition and rickets, so he didn't grow properly and had been left with one leg about two inches shorter than the other. Worse, he had been beaten before he was abandoned, so badly that the authorities believed his parents thought they had killed him—that's probably why they abandoned him. There was no cartilage in his nose and he suffered some slight brain damage—he had a *lot* of problems. But he also had the greatest smile you've ever seen and the most incredible outlook on life; he was one of the most loving kids you could ever hope to know.

We were expecting one new sibling and we got two. Mom was always full of surprises.

Dusty didn't seem to mind Dodie, she was just one more girl in his young life. But when he first laid eyes on Sandy, he asked, "How long is *he* going to be here?" Despite what Mom thought, I don't believe that Dusty had ever felt the lack of a little brother or any brother, period. He seemed to like being the only boy. So at first he and Sandy had some real problems. Then, as Dad liked to tell the story, he took the two boys on a fishing trip and by the time they all got back things had become much better and the boys were well on the road to being real brothers.

As with most siblings, though, there was a leader and a follower. Dusty was the leader and the one who thought up things to do and Sandy, bless his heart, was the one who did the "doing" and got in trouble. He thought Dusty was absolutely wonderful and could never say no to anything Dusty devised. Sandy hadn't been with us very long before Dusty got the idea that the barn at the back of our property needed painting. Of course, he got this idea when he spotted cans of paint stored in the barn. He found brushes in Dad's garage up at the house and soon he and Sandy were well on their way to earning a union card. Dusty knew about what time Dad would be getting home, so around that time he left Sandy and headed up to the house for a bathroom stop. When Dad got home, he found a clean Dusty watching TV in the family room and Sandy with a red paint brush in his hands working away on the barn.

You could multiply the mischief whenever Rex Allen would bring his boys over. Rex Jr. (Chico) and Dusty were the same age and their younger brothers Curt and Sandy were perfect foils for the two older brothers they idolized. What Chico didn't think of, Dusty did, and the younger two followed along. Of course, the Dads did know who the leaders were.

In 1954, Mom and Dad toured Scotland, Ireland, and England with the Reverend Billy Graham. While performing in Edinburgh, Scotland, they were visited backstage by a group of children from Dunforth Orphanage. The Chief Constable of Edinburgh is the Queen's representative and the top law officer for Scotland. At that time, William Merrilees was the chief constable. He and his wife had taken a young girl named Marion McGinnis Fleming under their wing. Marion was, as she would say, a "wee young lass" of 13. She could dance a delightful Irish jig and had a sweet, wistful singing voice. "Uncle Willie" asked her to sing for Mom and Dad. They immediately fell in love with her and invited her to spend the summer in the States.

Mom and Dad were always trying to find children for their friends and family members to adopt. They must have found three or four (at least) children for Pat and Fayetta Brady. The children all had bright red hair (as did both Pat and Fayetta) and no one but Pat or Fayetta would have known they had been adopted. They also were constantly on the lookout for children for Mom's brother, Hillman Smith Jr., and his wife, Bennie Merle, to adopt. Never mind that neither couple had asked Mom or Dad to do this. They were just so happy adopting that they thought everyone should do it.

This time, they hoped their close friends, and Dad's merchandising manager, Larry and Dorothy Kent, might adopt Marion. Poor Larry and Dorothy only had one daughter and a beautiful large home, so Mom reasoned that they *must* need another child to complete their family. By the time they learned of the legal roadblocks to an adoption, Marion was already in the States.

Also, Mimi (as we soon began calling her) had been raised with a bunch of kids in an orphanage and although Larry and Dorothy had a beautiful home, their lifestyle was very formal and sedate. Our house was at the opposite extreme—I think "rough-and-tumble" would sum it up pretty well. That kind of chaos isn't for everybody but it seemed to suit Mimi very well— maybe she liked the fact that it was filled with kids and nonstop action. No matter, the "fit" was perfect. She seemed a lot more comfortable with us and, once she spent a couple of weeks with us, we just couldn't stand the thought of her leaving us and going back to Scotland. So Mom talked to Mr. Merrilees.

While Mom and Dad couldn't adopt Mimi, he was able to arrange for her to stay in the United States on a student visa. When we were seniors in high school, she married one of our classmates and many years later she finally acquired U.S. citizenship.

Next, Mom decided that Dodie needed a sister who would be closer to her in age. She was worried that Dodie, with her dark skin, hair, and eyes, might later feel like the odd man out. At the time, Mom and Dad were sponsoring twelve Korean orphans through a couple of different agencies. Mom got pictures of several of them from World Vision and picked out the one she thought was closest to Dodie in age and looks.

My 16th birthday was the most memorable I've ever had. I got my driver's license and a new little sister on the same day. Debbie was the best present I ever received. Now, I do realize that she wasn't meant especially for me—her plane just happened to arrive on that day. But I considered her my very special present.

She was four years old when we met her plane at LAX. We were enchanted when our beautiful Asian doll was carried off the plane. Poor little girl, she must have thought she had landed on an alien planet. The family had been shooting a commercial for Nestle's Quik that day. We had on lots of pancake makeup—I know the people at the DMV had sure been impressed earlier that day when I got my license!—and we were wearing our Western outfits.

We picked Debbie up at the airport during our lunch break and took her back to the studio with us so that we could complete shooting the commercial. I think she would have been stunned anyway, even if we hadn't looked so peculiar. She had just made a trans-Pacific flight, had been handed over to total strangers who spoke no Korean while she spoke no English. But she could sing, "Jesus a-loves a-me, this I-a know." Of course, she had no idea what it meant, but it was a charming song, which she tried to sing exactly as the missionaries had taught it to her.

Every time Debbie opened her mouth to speak, someone picked her up and rushed her off to a bathroom because we had no idea what the word for "potty" was in Korean. Thank heavens, waiting at home were James and Betty Ordano who worked for us as handyman and cook. Betty was Choctaw and African American, James was Filipino—and, to everyone's surprise, he spoke Korean! What a lucky break for us all—especially Debbie. James could communicate with her and she finally got most of the important words down. In fact, she did way better at learning English than any of us did at learning Korean, I'm embarrassed to say.

Language experts speak of the immersion technique; how if you just drop somebody in an environment they will learn the language very quickly. Debbie was absolutely amazing and pretty well proved the theory. She was only four years old and probably had only been with us a month when she was trying to tell Mom something apparently of great import to her. Mom tried but couldn't understand, causing Debbie no end of frustration. Mom said that Debbie stomped her little foot in utter disgust and, I swear, within a couple of months, Debbie stopped speaking Korean altogether. She wouldn't speak it at all, not even with James. She learned English almost overnight and she didn't even speak with an accent.

But that first day, when we pulled up to the house, two of our dogs came out to meet us. Debbie literally scaled the adults around her trying to get up high enough so the dogs couldn't get to her. We couldn't imagine what had terrified her so badly— neither Bowzer nor Bullet would hurt anyone. It wasn't until James asked Debbie about her reaction that we learned about her life in Korea and understood her fright. Where Debbie had come from, dogs were trained to hunt down the orphans that roamed the streets looking for food in garbage cans.

Oddly, for all the mixing and matching in our family, I don't remember much tension between the "old" kids and the "new" kids. We all got along well, and accepted each other very quickly. But that doesn't mean there weren't a few bumps in the road.

In general, we got along as well as any very big family with huge age differences, and probably a lot better than most. We had different tastes, different friends, and different interests, all gathered under one roof. Luckily, when we moved out to Chatsworth after Robin died, our new house was big enough to absorb us all and allow each of us to have a little elbow room. The house was almost two hundred feet long and sat on 141 acres, which afforded a lot of opportunities for solitude.

Since there were so many of us, Mom had built-in babysitters. When I was in high school, I remember sitting for Dodie and Debbie when the housekeeper had time off. I didn't sit for Mimi, Linda, or the boys. Linda was away at school my senior year, Mimi and I were the same age and she usually had her own plans, and the boys were just too uncontrollable—Mom would always make other arrangements for them.

The one bad thing about our age differences is that they sometimes prevented us from having the closeness normally associated with brothers and sisters. Dusty and Sandy were two schools removed from me; I was graduating from high school and worked after school and on weekends when they were in the fifth grade and the little girls were just starting kindergarten—you don't get very close under those conditions.

Besides, I was viewed as the older sister and an ogre. As adults, six years or even twelve years don't mean that much, but that's practically an entire generation to a child. It wasn't until Dodie was in high school that I realized that I never got, or took, the opportunity to really get to know her. She had been six when I left home and got married and only twelve when the family moved up to Apple Valley.

When our entire extended family still lived in the San Fernando Valley, I was at Mom and Dad's quite frequently. Mom and I belonged to a group of ladies that helped multiracial orphans and abused children. But once the folks moved to Apple Valley, I saw them much less often.

After a family gathering in Apple Valley, I realized that I didn't really even know Dodie. All of a sudden she was in high school—she had completely grown up in my absence. Outside of family get-togethers, I don't remember us socializing—the twelve-year difference in our ages has been tough to overcome.

Now, I'm happy to say, we are making up for lost time, thanks to our common interest in the equestrian unit I put together to ride in the Pasadena Tournament of Roses Parade. Dodie and I are finally friends and are trying to catch up on all the years we have lost. I have come to appreciate her as a sister and as a person. It is a pleasure to see what a bright, capable lady she has become—but it has taken some years for us to get to this point!

I have left Tom until last because, even though he's my older brother, he never lived with us. Tom was already in college when Mom and Dad married.

When I was younger, I was always in awe of Tommy. Mom bragged about him all the time, naturally. He's a wonderful musician who showed great promise when he was just a youngster. He composed and arranged the music for his high school graduation, as well as for his graduation from the University of Southern California where he received his Masters in Music degree, magna cum laude. As a teacher, his bands and orchestras have won awards everywhere he has taught. He's been a Minister of Music for some of the biggest churches in Sacramento and has led the joint choirs of Sacramento in their holiday programs for years. He finally retired last year and I hope this means that we will be able to spend more time together.

He married the only girl he ever went with, Barbara. She is a music teacher but also has a degree in physical education from UCLA. She's the perfect wife and mother to three great girls— now wives and mothers themselves. To me, a less-than-perfect teenage girl, they were a very daunting couple.

I finally got to know Tom and Barbara a lot better the last few years of Mom and Dad's lives when Larry and I moved to the high desert so that I could work for the museum and we could enable Mom and Dad to stay active. Tom and Barbara had provided a home for her aging mother the last years of her life and they were well aware of the changes that Mom and Dad would soon encounter. Because we were at Mom and Dad's just about every day, we were able to spend time with Tom and Barbara on their frequent visits from Sacramento.

It wasn't until the last couple of years that I have come to know the eldest and youngest of my siblings for the wonderful, warm people they are. It's a shame that we lived so many years before we got to know each other better. But in most ways, I truly believe that our many differences helped pull us together more than they created problems.

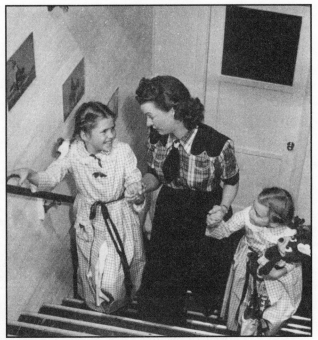

Linda Lou and I go up stairs with our new Mom, wearing the robes we modeled in the fashion show at Gale Patrick's kids shop. (1948)

Reverend Jack MacArthur greets the new Rogers family at the door of Fountain Avenue Baptist Church in Hollywood. (1948)

It was an accident, Mom! (1949)

Mom, Dusty, Linda Lou and I greet Dad and Trigger while we await our ride at the Hollywood Santa Claus Lane Parade (1953)

Me, Dad, Linda Lou, Mimi, Sandy and Dusty gather around the pickup that Dad and Grampy drove from Duck Run, OH to California.

Mom, Sandy, Dusty and Linda Lou join me at the piano. (1952)

On the set of *Under California Stars* with Andy Devine and Dad. (194?)

Most kids have a little red wagon but I had a little red stage-coach that we used in the Santa Claus Lane Parade a couple of times. (Dad, Mom, Linda, Dusty and me)

Dusty meets his new brother (Sandy) and baby sister (Dodie) when they arrive at Los Angeles Airport (Oct., 1952).

Dad fixing my bike. (1951)

Front view of the Chatsworth house. We lived there from 1955 to 1964.

Mimi, Dusty and I wait behind the grandstand to join the rest of the family at one of many state fairs where we performed. (1955)

Dad and me at the Egyptian Theater for the premier of *King Richard and the Crusaders*. (1954)

Visiting Dad's childhood home in Duck Run, OH. Dad was so proud of the fact that he and Grampy built the house.

Dad sat me on a saddle at an early age. (1941)

Dad plays horsey with Linda Lou and me. (1945)

Dad and Linda Lou turn the rope for me in the backyard of the house on Longridge. (1946)

Dad shows Linda and me how to use a rope. This photo was taken at Glenn Randall's stables in Van Nuys where Trigger was trained and stabled. (1946)

Linda and me
with Dusty in
his Christening
gown. (1946)

Hope Cottage, Dallas, Texas,
where I was born and Dad found me.

A rare shot of
Mommy (Arline)
wearing western
clothes (1940).

The three of us with one of Dad's motorcycles in front of the White Oak house. (1942)

My first piano lesson. (1941)

Don Reynolds and me on our ponies at Glenn Randall's ranch in Van Nuys. Don was called "Jug" or "Little Brown Jug" when he acted in movies (he was one of the kids who played Little Beaver in the Red Ryder films). He was acting in movies and doing his own stunts when he was still in rompers.

George "Gabby" Hayes has always been one of my favorite people. He also helped spoil me by letting me comb his beard. He's dressed the way I remember him best, custom made silk shirt and British suit. (1944)

With Dale Robertson at
a Western film festival
in the gold country
of California. (1997)

Larry and me with Republic
star (and the last of the "Singing
Cowboys") Monte Hale. I have
loved Monte since I was a little
girl and he took me to church
one Sunday that Dad and
Mommy were out of town.

Waving to the crowd at the
1999 Pasadena Tournament
of Roses Parade. The outfit
I am wearing is one that
Nudie made for Mom when
she and Dad were the
Grand Marshalls in the 1970s

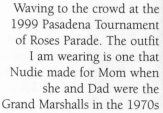

Similar outfit but without the horse and just a few years in between. (1947)

My high school graduation portrait.

Larry and I were married in the living room of Mom and Dad's Apple Valley house on Dec. 27, 1981.

Mary and Bill Newhouse, Larry's mom and dad, Larry, me, Rev. Bill Hansen, pastor of Church of the Valley Presbyterian in Apple Valley, and Mom and Dad.

Rex Allen, Jr. and I
have known each other
since he was a little kid.

Backstage with the
Riders in the Sky, one
of my favorite groups.
Woody, Too Slim
and Ranger Doug.

Meeting Ricky Skaggs,
one of the greatest
Bluegrass musicians ever.

This photo was taken at the last Golden Boot Awards Dad attended in 1997. He and Mom had a great time that evening and I was privileged to join them. (Photograph by Roger Karnbad and by permission of the Motion Picture and Television Fund)

One of the crew took this candid photo of the Rogers family at Big Bear Lake where we joined Mom and Dad on location for *The Roy Rogers Show*. Dad, Dusty, Sandy, Mimi with Debbie, Linda with Dodie, me and Mom. (1956)

9

Another Family

I **hope it's obvious** that I've always adored my parents. But like many adopted kids, I became curious early on as to the identity of my birth mother. Mom completely supported me in this but Dad often wondered why I wanted to know. I tried explaining to him that it was my birth mother I was looking for, not another father. I don't know if I would have been so curious if Mommy had lived. I don't know if my several years of estrangement with Mom fueled my search. I only know that as I entered my teens, finding my birth mother became more and more important to me.

The summer I was twelve, I went to Dallas on a visit with friends of Dad. They were the people who made the Roy Rogers boots and they had an adopted daughter my age and an adopted daughter Linda Lou's age. Both of their girls had come from Hope Cottage. When they invited me to stay with them in Dallas, Mom asked them if they minded taking me over to Hope Cottage so I could see where I had "come from." The woman who had supervised my adoption was still running the place, and I took the opportunity to ask her about my birth mother. But, of course, she couldn't tell me anything. Texas was one of the states that was absolutely closed as far as adoption records go.

When I got back home, Mom and I had a long mother-daughter talk about why I felt the need to find my birth mother. She really made me think about what would be the best outcome I could hope for and what I would do if the outcome was not what I wanted. She was a terrific counselor with great common sense, very down to earth. She said, "I really want you to think about this and if you decide that you want to do it, I will help you any way that I can. But I want you to understand that things might not turn out exactly as you hope."

She told me about a gentleman that she worked with some years earlier who had found his birth mother, and it turned out she was living in New Orleans in a "sporting house." Even though he was in his early thirties and very successful, the revelation disturbed him deeply and he had a nervous breakdown.

Mom told me this because she knew that, like so many adopted kids, I used to make up stories about my "real" parents. My mother was a Spanish Princess, or a gypsy, or a star on Broadway. My father was an English prince, a soldier, a gypsy, and even though it was "true love," their parents or guardians had forced them apart. Since my story tended to change depending on the previous weekend's Saturday matinee, my little friends must have thought I was a bit weird to not know who my parents were.

So Mom told me to hope for the best but to be prepared for the worst. "If you can accept that," she said, "*really* accept it and you still want to do it, I will help you find your birth mother." And she did.

Mom had influential friends all over Texas. She now used some of those friendships to get information about my birth mother. I was twenty-four years old when we were finally able to locate my birth family.

The first person I contacted was my birth grandfather. I was sensitive to the idea that my mother might not have told her current husband of my existence, so I wrote my grandfather to ask if he thought it would be okay for me to contact my mother. He wrote back that he was happy to hear from me and had wondered for years where I was and how had I been raised. He also said that he would be happy to give my mother a letter from me.

I immediately contacted him by phone to ask about the circumstances of my adoption. He explained that when my teenage mother found out she was pregnant, her older sister had just been widowed and had returned to their parents' home with four small children. My grandfather was a carpenter in a little town in East Texas and the Texas economy had still not recovered from the Depression. My mother had been engaged but suddenly decided that she didn't want to get married. As my grandfather told me twenty-four years later, "When she made that decision, I felt I had no other choice. We just couldn't take on another mouth to feed." My grandparents still had younger children of their own at home. So he made inquiries and then drove my mother to Hope Cottage when it was time to have her baby. He said that he had always felt a little guilty about forcing the decision on her and was relieved to know that I held no grudge against any of them and actually wanted to get to know them.

I wrote my mother, telling her a little about my life up to then, my large family, my marriage, everything. I did not, however, tell anyone who my adoptive parents were. After exchanging several letters, I traveled to Texas to meet my new family: my mother, grandfather, aunts and uncles, several half sisters and several half brothers—as if I didn't already belong to a large family!

I finally told them who had adopted me and asked them if they had ever wondered if I was the baby adopted by Roy Rogers and his first wife. They told me that it had never occurred to them. Hope Cottage's policy was to not tell the mothers if they had given birth to a boy or girl, feeling that the mother wouldn't have as hard a time living with her decision if she couldn't even attach a gender to the baby she had given up for adoption. They had no idea if she had given birth to a boy or a girl, and I wasn't officially adopted until several months following my birth. Even though they knew Roy Rogers had adopted a baby from Hope Cottage, they had never made the connection.

I have since made an effort to contact my birth father, but he wanted no contact and I have respected his wishes.

I tell this story because I come across a lot of adopted children and adults at various outings and events. Because of my being a Rogers, they want to know if I am one of the adopted kids and, if so, if I ever traced my birth family.

Truthfully, I have never regretted tracing my birth mother. We have never become very close. But I have gotten to know and establish a bond with my sisters. They are lovely women who have raised wonderful families of their own. I have never really gotten to know any of my brothers very well; they're much younger than I am and we have no shared experiences upon which to build a relationship.

I am very close to my one half sister. I try to visit her whenever I'm in the Dallas area and we talk often on the telephone. We have gotten to be really good friends. She's a couple of years younger than I am and though we were raised half a continent apart and have different fathers, we are similar in many ways, even to sharing some of the same health concerns, and even look quite a bit alike. We are also very much alike in our temperaments. This is a source of constant teasing by our husbands.

In any case, I'm glad that I was able to track my mother down, learn of her life, and fill in some of the blanks in my life. My only regret is that I didn't locate them all the prior year when my grandmother was still alive. I understand that she was a really nice lady and I wish I had been able to meet her. However, I am very glad that I did have the chance to meet and get to know my wonderful grandfather. I was able to have several more visits and conversations with him, and I prize every visit we had.

10

Back to School

There is a section in *Happy Trails,* Mom and Dad's auto-biography, where reference is made to a trip we took to Canada for the Canadian National Exhibition in Toronto the summer I was fourteen. Since I was older and had been working very hard at my singing and lobbying even harder, Mom and Dad had given me a couple of numbers to perform in the show. But Dad goes on to relate how I "came down with a serious case of show business fever" and that I was suddenly receiving a lot of attention from boys in the audience. He further states that "Cheryl matter-of-factly informed us that she was eagerly looking forward to" performing with them at Madison Square Garden in September. Supposedly, I threw a fit and did the mistreated teenager routine when told I couldn't go because of school. And that the minute we all got home, I went next door to the neighbors proclaiming I was leaving home forever.

This is a highly revised and glossed-over period in my life that was actually a real crisis for me. Several factors were at work: I was a rapidly developing teenager who looked and acted much older than I was. I was striving for independence—to be the adult I felt I had already become. There were still unresolved issues going all the way back to when, after Mommy died, Dad told me I was in charge of my siblings and that he really depended upon me. I had really taken that responsibility to heart and it profoundly affected me when Mom came in and took over my job. And I still hadn't gotten over the loss of Robin.

Our early housekeepers had created additional complications as they favored Dusty—after all, he was an infant when they arrived and they considered him their child—and let him get away with murder. He was a typical little brother, and *I* was usually held responsible for his mischief. It seemed to me that he understood this and delighted in using it—like I said, a typical little brother. He has written and said many times that I used to make him furious because I would pull his hair. He often uses this in his stage act and jokes that I am the cause of his thinning hair. But, to show it works both ways, I have the scars on my shins from his retaliation. And, on top of this, my brothers and sisters called me "Queenie" in response to what they saw as my bossiness.

I was in a lot of torment and was full of conflicts. Mom and I clashed, and though I loved her dearly and admired her greatly, I still, at times, viewed her as an interloper. When she tried to discuss things with me and asked me to be patient, I would grow up soon enough, I took great delight in pointing out to her that she was already married at my age.

What really happened is this: Mom and Dad still had another week of performances left in Toronto when I had to leave to start school at Corvallis High School. Mom and Dad were going to proceed to New York for a week of rehearsals and two weeks of performances.

Shortly after I returned from Canada, our housekeeper Virginia Peck (the one who thought she was Dusty's mother) and I got into a serious disagreement. I went to a neighbor's house, borrowed a phone to call Father Smith, and asked him to come get me. I talked to him about what was going on with me. He was a former schoolteacher and a psychologist. I guess he thought the situation warranted his taking some action. He telephoned Mom and Dad in New York and told them he thought it best that I go away to school for a while and that he would give them a list of schools from which to pick within a couple of days.

The upshot of all this was that in October of 1954, just as Mom and Dad finished their show in New York, I was on my way to Kemper Hall, an Episcopal convent in Kenosha, Wisconsin. Father Smith and Mom thought Kenosha would be far enough away from Hollywood that I could, for once, be anonymous and find room to grow from child to woman without the press looking at my every move. Mom met me at O'Hare Airport in Chicago and accompanied me on the "el" train to Kenosha. During the trip, I told her that I thought it was obvious that I wasn't needed at home and that I was planning on staying in the Midwest until I graduated from college.

When we arrived at the school, we discovered that the day's headlines in the local newspaper read, "Daughter of Roy Rogers and Dale Evans to attend Kemper." This rather upset Mom and proved an embarrassment to the nuns, who were very protective of the privacy of all their girls. They were at a loss to understand how the newspaper learned of the story. Ah, the joys of being a celebrity kid!

Even though going away to school had been my choice, it was rough adjusting to being so far away from home. Villa Cabrini had only been about a half hour's drive from Hollywood, but Kenosha was half a *continent* away.

As was the case throughout my life, the first friends I made weren't in my class, they were upperclassmen. My classmates put up with this for just so long; then they sat me down and explained that they expected me to spend more of my time with them. After a change in my behavior, I felt more accepted.

I really liked the atmosphere at Kemper Hall. The classes, the teachers, and the assignments all provided the challenges I needed and I thrived in the stable environment. At the time it was ranked the No. 1 girls' school in the country for academics. I made friends there that I'm still in touch with today.

My sister Linda Lou, however, went there a couple of years later and she hated it. But that was her first and only experience with boarding school and must have been a considerable culture shock for her.

I spent the holidays with the families of friends I made there: Thanksgiving with my roommate JoAnna's family, Christmas at my friend Sharon's, and Easter was spent partly in Chicago with my friend Kay and her mom, and partly at Great Lakes Naval Base. Jean McLean was one of my classmates and her father was captain at Great Lakes. She invited several of us to spend part of the Easter holiday with her family. It was amazing—a three-story mansion staffed by Filipino sailors—and a whole Naval base full of young men. Even though we were never allowed outside her house without an escort, what an exciting couple of days for a bunch of fourteen-year-old girls!

The rest of Easter vacation was spent with Mom and Dad at the governor's mansion in Tennessee. Mom and Dad were again presenting the safety awards, this time just outside Nashville, and they asked me to join them. The governor was quite young and he and his family were extremely hospitable. He was trying to bring about prison reform in his state, which we later learned was a very controversial issue. We attended a luncheon and a dinner and I got to see some of the Southern politicians who were making the headlines at the time—the politicians who were mostly for segregation. This was a really alien concept to me. I grew up in Hollywood where talent was what set you apart, or so I always thought. Remember, teenagers are usually very idealistic.

Unfortunately, I was able to stay at Kemper Hall for only one school year. Then I had to return home to California. It was Dad's decision that I return home, and I thought at the time that he was just being arbitrary. I later learned that it was a decision dictated by economics. Dad was producing his own television series and extensively renovating an older, historic ranch house. Unnecessary expenses had to be cut.

That summer of 1955, the family moved to Chatsworth, where Dad had purchased a 141-acre ranch where he planned to produce television shows, including his own *Roy Rogers Show*.

One of my most traumatic experiences occurred while I still had my learner's permit. I didn't have my own car, "Gertrude the Gutless Wonder," yet and was still driving Dad's back-up Jeep, Jezebel. I found it mortifying to be the only girl that drove a Jeep to school until I discovered that the boys thought it was really cool—then it wasn't quite so bad. Anyway, one Saturday afternoon, Mimi and I, along with three or four other Chatsworth girls, decided to go to Bob's Big Boy. As long as we paid for our own gas, didn't have any boys with us, and I wasn't on restriction, Mom didn't mind if we drove into Van Nuys—but, I had to have a licensed driver with me because of the learner's permit. I was only a week or so away from getting my license and I had been driving just about every day. We had several girlfriends who had licenses but no car—so I could almost always find someone that had a license to go with us. This time though, no one was available.

Well, by now I was confident that I was a good driver and nothing would go wrong. We had traversed the West Valley without incident and were heading south on Van Nuys Boulevard when the light in front of us turned red. I slowed to a stop well behind the line and everything was fine until I glanced behind me—there was a black & white with two young police officers eyeing this green Jeep full of teenage girls.

Horrors! I was sure they knew I didn't have a licensed driver with me! The light turned green, I smoothly put Jezebel into gear, stepped on the gas, and backed right into the police car!!! I wanted to die. I hoped to die—there was no way to explain this to Mom. I again looked in my rearview mirror and the officers must have seen my bright red face because they appeared to be doubled over in laughter at my predicament. Luckily, I had only eased my foot onto the gas pedal and we had only tapped the police car. I immediately put Jezebel into the correct gear—forward this time—made a right-hand turn and headed back to Chatsworth—forthwith. The last glimpse I had of those officers, they were still doubled over laughing at me.

I couldn't wait to get my driver's license. Dad had recently spent $500 of my hard-earned money to buy Gertrude. I was working at a dress shop in Canoga Park and we lived in Chatsworth. You *were not late* for dinner at the Rogers house. Dinner went on the table at 6:00, period. It didn't make any difference if it was Dad who was late, or one of us kids, dinner was served at 6:00 because Mom had a schedule.

One afternoon, I had to work a few minutes late. I'd only had my license maybe two weeks and I was going to be late for dinner, so I started speeding down Canoga Avenue and suddenly I heard a siren behind me. Busted! When I got home with that ticket, Mom was very angry. She went to Van Nuys with me, to traffic court. I didn't argue or make any excuse, I had been speeding. Because it was my first ticket, the judge suspended my license for four weeks—but Mom, a much sterner judge, held it for three months! That really cramped my style. I had two jobs after school—so for those three months I had to be very persistent and creative in detecting anyone who was going in my direction and begging a ride. I haven't gotten a speeding ticket since then.

Mimi and I were enrolled in Canoga Park High School which, with only about 1,400 students, was the smallest high school in the Los Angeles School District. This was one of my better school experiences. There were some very good teachers, I met some schoolmates who became lifelong friends, and I met by future husband. I was able to get my learner's permit and then my driver's license shortly after we started the new semester. Finally, independence!

The next year, thanks to Kemper, I found that I had more than enough credits to graduate a whole semester early. In fact, I could have graduated a whole year early but I needed one class, Senior Problems. Mom finally decided that it was silly for me to be taking Bookkeeping I and lower division classes just to fill a desk, and she gave me permission to accelerate and graduate in the winter '58 class.

There were still some minor incidents at school stemming from my famous parentage, but I mostly enjoyed Canoga, its faculty and students. The last remaining problem was that I still felt like an adult trapped in a teenager's body.

𝄢

A Child of Celebrity

𝓘**am often asked** when it was that I first realized my Dad didn't have an average job. The answer is, I think I always knew. Even in elementary school I knew that Dad didn't do the same job that my friend Iris's father did. He was a plumber and probably made more money than Dad at the time! While on the Republic lot, I saw electricians, carpenters, and the like. I knew that Dad was part of that workforce but he was treated differently than the crew. So I didn't have to think very hard to figure out that he did something very special.

Whether it was because of the tragedies in our family, Mom and Dad's Christian stand, or their publicly voiced patriotism, people seemed to have strong feelings regarding my parents and us kids. They either seemed predisposed to see us as the ideal American Family and expect only the best of us, or they looked for the extreme and sensational.

Going to school in the San Fernando Valley was wonderful because so many of the kids I went to school with had parents in show business. I think we all were afforded a great deal of leeway and protection because the studios played such a large economic role in the area where we lived. The kids I attended class with were the kids of actors, grips, and soundmen, or their dads worked in the accounting or casting office of a studio. Hollywood and the Valley were pretty small when I was growing up; there were only around 300,000 people in the San Fernando Valley in the late '40s.

At Longridge Nursery School I attended class with the sons of Dick Haines and Jack Carson, who lived diagonally across the street from us. I didn't actually go to school with Susan Hayward's twin sons because they were a little younger than I was, but she lived directly across the street from us on Longridge in Studio City. The family of Lou Costello—the short, cuddly, wonderful half of Abbott and Costello—lived down the street from us and there were two daughters about my age.

When we moved to Encino in the early '50s, the daughter of Duncan Renaldo, the "Cisco Kid," was in my class, as was the daughter of Bud Abbott, the other half of Abbott and Costello.

The irony is that some people treated us as if we were snobby rich kids simply because our parents were movie stars; it's ironic because we weren't rich at all—our folks worked for Republic, one of the "poverty row" studios, not MGM or Paramount. Don't get me wrong, we weren't poor by any means, but I never saw evidence of us being rich, with the possible exception of Dad's toys. But most of them had been given to him so people could say that Roy Rogers used their product. Even if we had been rich, I don't think Mom or Dad would have lived any differently. They were extremely unpretentious, down-to-earth people and they expected us to be the same way.

That wasn't difficult, since we all had to earn our own spending money and what clothes Mom *did* buy us usually came from bargain tables. She wouldn't buy anything that wasn't on sale. I think it was a habit she formed during the Depression and while a single, working mother.

Mimi and I got $5.00 allowance when we were in high school. That $5.00 was for gas, incidentals at school, snacks, and after-school activities. For that, we had to do chores around the house; neither Mom nor Dad would just hand us money. If we wanted more than $5.00 we were expected to earn it by doing either extra chores at home or getting an outside job.

I don't remember Dad spending lots of money on anything other than hunting dogs, guns, and other guy toys. There were no limos in our lifestyle, no extravagance. Mom and Dad rarely went to Hollywood parties unless they were charity affairs. Our folks were models of good, solid Midwestern Christian values.

My husband Larry likes to say that I grew up like your average middle-class American family of very famous parents. Our home had strong Midwestern values, the values that Mom and Dad had learned growing up. Mom grew up in a Southern Baptist family with the values that were very much prevalent in her generation. When she was a teenager, she really rebelled. . . . She just wanted to be in the entertainment business and that was definitely different from how she had been raised. When she married Dad and had all of us kids, she reverted to what she knew. We went to church *every* Sunday and sometimes to several services. I sang in the choir and played piano for Sunday school. By the time I was in high school I would go back for the evening service and play piano for that.

Wednesday night was choir practice. My sister Mimi and I would pile into Gertrude the Gutless Wonder and fly down from Chatsworth into Van Nuys to Bob's Big Boy to spend ten minutes there so we could get a cherry coke and an order of French fries. We knew we didn't dare be late and have to tell her what we had been doing. Mom had all of these formulas: you had so long after choir practice before you had to be in the driveway. If you went to the drive-in movie you had so long from when that movie ended and when you had to be in the driveway. She would check in the paper to see when the movie ended; she always checked and we knew it. If I was supposed to be home at 11:30, at 11:30 *exactly* Mom had her finger on the intercom button to my bedroom, saying, "Cheryl are you there?", and I'd better *be* there! The whole house was wired for sound, by the way.

In some ways, because our parents were such role models, we were held to a higher standard of behavior than most celebrity kids. After I had my driver's license, if I went speeding up the hill toward home or if I got home late, the neighbors would be on the phone to Mom immediately, or they would tell her at church on Sunday.

Mom and Dad themselves weren't really preachy, but our housekeepers were always telling us, "You should get down on your knees every day and thank God for the parents you have." And the grandparents would join in, "You should never be seen with someone or somewhere that will reflect badly on your parents." We took this advice to heart and tried our best to never publicly embarrass our parents.

There are a lot of people who have preconceived ideas of how a movie star's child behaves, and at times it was very difficult to live up to that or avoid living down to it. I was very independent and tried to not let other people's expectations dictate what I would or would not do.

It seemed easier to fit in when attending school in the San Fernando Valley where there were lots of movie kids. But attending a high school in Kenosha, Wisconsin, was different. Very different. Believe me, there were no kids connected to the movie industry there. Only me. And that made me stand out like the proverbial sore thumb.

Like when the headlines of that newspaper announced my presence at Kemper Hall. That did not start things off on the right foot. Almost from the beginning, it seemed that there were people in the town who were determined to think the worst of me, for no other reason than that I was who I was. A week or so after we had returned from Christmas holidays, which I spent with my girlfriend Sharon in Hammond, Indiana, we were in our school blazers walking down the street in Kenosha with one of the nuns (freshmen weren't allowed off campus without a nun escort). Two ladies spotted us and started talking to each other about that awful daughter of Roy Rogers. One of the women said, "She was here at a Christmas party and she was drunk!"—keep in mind that I was fourteen years old at the time.

I walked up to the women and said, "I happen to know that Cheryl Rogers was away for the Christmas holiday."

They looked at me like they knew I was lying. One of them defiantly said, "No she wasn't, she was here and she was drunk!"

Several of the girls, not wanting to give me away, said that, no, they were pretty sure she had gone away for the holidays.

I asked her what this Cheryl Rogers looked like.

"She is about 5'6" and blonde," the woman replied.

"No," I said, calmly, "she's about my height (5'4") and my coloring (brunette)."

Now the two women were convinced I was lying! I considered taking out my I.D. but I don't think they would have believed even that—they so desperately wanted to think the worst. Finally, tired of the argument, both women called us liars and huffed off down the street.

Something similar happened about a year later shortly after I transferred to Canoga Park High School. Walking out of the science building one day, I followed a couple of girls down the steps. They looked back at me, smiled and said hello—then went back to their conversation about that awful Cheryl Rogers and what a snob she was. They clearly had no idea who I was—I was walking right behind them; they knew I was there, but they didn't have a clue as to who I was.

That kind of thing didn't happen all the time of course, but it happened often enough and it was always hurtful. For Linda Lou and Dusty, I think it was even more hurtful because they were both so shy. Even though instances like these upset me at the time, I was brash enough to shrug them off and think to myself, "Well, they obviously don't know who I am, so why get upset about it?" I guess that's the kind of attitude that kept me from doing crazy and destructive things like some celebrities' kids seemed prone to do.

There were times when being the daughter of famous parents could have major drawbacks, just because of their celebrity.

Mom, for the most part, could often move about in public without causing too much of a stir but Dad got absolutely mobbed. He never took me to a father/daughter event at school and I guess it was for that reason. I asked him every time, but he was never available.

Because he was performing at a rodeo in Houston, Dad didn't attend my high school graduation, even though I was one of the two valedictorians of my class. Looking back I'm almost surprised that he attended our weddings, but he wouldn't have dared miss one of those—Mom would have killed him.

But all in all—for me, at least—the good parts about being a Rogers far outweighed the bad. Given my personality and temperament, I was able to really enjoy it, even love it at times. That's because I could get some *reflection* of the spotlight without the heat of the real thing. What I mean is that I loved being *part* of it but not being *of* it.

Even after I was married, I could volunteer and help set up shows for luncheons, dinners or other fundraisers; call on my friends, as well as some of Mom and Dad's; and get them to volunteer to help the cause, whatever it might be. One year I was at KCET and helped bring in some of the auctioneers, then I was asked to do the greenroom briefing, and the assistant director got sick and they asked me to take over a few of his duties—I had a ball. I loved working backstage. To me, those are the best jobs because you are an integral part of what's taking place, but you are anonymous when you leave to go home at night.

I had more than enough of reporters when I was a kid. They followed us around all the time when we were little. Our pictures were in the movie magazines every month.

And, if you believe the magazines, I even wrote some of the articles myself! People sometimes send me a copy of a magazine article from when I was a little girl, and there it is: "By Cheryl Rogers." Well, of *course* I didn't write the article—I was six or seven years old! I don't remember even talking to most of those reporters. It was a story the studio came up with and gave to the reporters or a situation the studio set up and just "happened" to have a reporter and photographer on hand. The articles would then list of my favorite movie stars or my favorite kiddie places to visit, but they were usually totally off.

Today there are advocate groups, particularly Paul Petersen's A Minor Affair, that try to protect child actors. Sometimes, I wonder if there shouldn't be something similar for the children of celebrities. It is true, we don't necessarily grow up in the full glare of the spotlight, but we are still illuminated by the reflected light of our parents.

And that could sometimes make for very exciting times.

When I was sixteen, Dad asked me to be a timekeeper for the annual San Pedro to Catalina Island Race. People used to race small boats across Catalina Channel from San Pedro to Avalon. Dad owned part of the Yellow Jacket Boat Company in Texas. He had been in the race several times and had won it a couple of times. This particular race, he and several of his friends were driving sixteen-foot Yellow Jackets. Among them were actors Dick Jones (*Young Buffalo Bill* and *The Range Rider*) and John Derek. John showed up on the day before the race with his girlfriend, Ursula Andress, one of the most beautiful women I have ever seen—and she was only nineteen at the time.

Ursula, Dick's wife, Betty, and the wives of a couple of Dad's other friends were to be with me aboard Dad's converted PT boat, the Flamba, which would serve as the floating headquarters for the race. There was a little light fog when we left San Pedro but the forecast called for it to burn off by mid-morning. Going across on the Flamba though, we ran into some very dense fog right in the middle of the channel. Dad's partner, Roger Cunningham, was our skipper and he reported the fogbank to the Coast Guard. They reported the race had already started and there was no way to contact the little boats. Obviously, there were no cell phones then. Dick Jones won the race that day. Dad arrived about fifteen minutes late—he had overshot the island but realized it almost immediately, turned around and found Catalina within minutes.

However, John Derek and Dad's good friend Ray Camp weren't found until the next day by the Coast Guard. They had run out of gas and floated almost to Mexico. While they were missing, it fell to me to make gallons and gallons of coffee for everybody as we stayed up all night waiting to hear news about our lost friends. That is, everybody stayed up except Dad, who had no doubts that they would be found safe and sound and went to bed at his regular time. Normally, it was Mom who made the coffee, and provided the comforting words, but she was in the hospital with an inner-ear infection so I got to be her stand-in. That was an exciting couple of days for me.

— — —

I won't speak for my sisters, but part of my drive to be an adult was because adults were independent, got to go where they wanted, do what they wanted, be seen with whomsoever they wanted. Not that I wanted to go anywhere, do anything or be seen with someone unacceptable—it was just the principle of the thing.

Celebrity kids can't be spontaneous. We were trained to think first about what kind of a reflection our actions would be on our parents. I don't remember Mom and Dad preaching this, but our grandparents, the people who worked for Mom and Dad, and our housekeepers were constantly reminding us that anything that we did could find its way into the newspapers or movie magazines (a fate worse than death—embarrassing the parents!).

Once I was married, I could finally choose to be a Rogers or not. I could still participate in charity events, public forums and even the very occasional TV show, but it was my choice to be Cheryl Rose or Cheryl Rogers—and as soon as the program was over, I could be anonymous again. Up until I was married, I didn't have that option.

In many ways, Mom was a bundle of contradictions. She always drilled it into our heads that girls should get married and have babies and grandchildren. When she got older she blamed the demise of the family on *Cosmopolitan* magazine. I would constantly point out to her that she had never been a stay-at-home Mom except for the couple of months when she was on suspension, and even then she would just go crazy trying to find something to do. This just wasn't her. She was an author and a songwriter and a performer—a career woman. But that's not what she wanted for her girls. She always talked about how much she had missed with Tommy and how much she regretted not being able to have him with her all the time because she had to work and earn the money to send home to her parents who were keeping him. She was really conflicted with all of that. She insisted that we all take secretarial classes because one never knew when one might have to go to work. The work ethic was always there and it was instilled in all of us, but for her daughters she wanted what she conceived as a traditional woman's role.

Now what a woman was supposed to do when the kids were grown and out of the house I have no idea, and I don't think

Mom knew either, because she never took time to take a deep breath. But that was how she raised us and what her vision of what her daughters' lives should be. That might be one of the big contributing factors as to why all of us married so early—because that's what we always heard from her.

Mom and Dad had chosen to be entertainers; we were celebrity kids from the get-go. My adoption had made the national newspapers and magazines. Whenever we entered a new school, there were always those who hated us or cozied up to us for who Mom and Dad were—not who we were. We always had to be careful when making friends. We had to keep in mind that even the most casual conversation—say, with someone sitting next to you on the bus—could find its way into print. In addition to all that, I tended to be overly dramatic (considering the things I've said up to now, this must come as a real surprise to you) and took myself very seriously. I was a good student who made excellent grades, worked outside school, often at two or three jobs at a time, loved dramatic movies, adored my horse . . . and often thought about killing myself.

I didn't talk about it, only to one or two of my very closest friends, but I thought about it often. Maybe it was just that I was a teenager, maybe it was some deeper issue that I didn't know how to deal with at the moment. Yet, despite those occasional dark thoughts—and I know that this will sound strange following the previous statement—I think I was fairly happy. I just hated being a teenager and wanted to be an adult. In the '50s, a girl accomplished this by being married.

12

Western Flash

Certain symbols are automatically associated with Mom and Dad—Trigger, *Happy Trails*, Buttermilk, Nellybelle, and flashy clothes.

Around the house, Dad was most comfortable in tennis shoes, jeans, and either a T-shirt or no shirt at all. Mom never seemed to care much what she wore when she wasn't working.

I used to tease her that on the days she wasn't working, she went into her closet, stuck out her hand, and whatever it touched first was what she put on. She would have on a pink flowered skirt and an orange and yellow plaid shirt—and she wasn't even color blind!

Dad, I think, could be credited with inspiring the term "rhinestone cowboy," based on his colorful outfits. There are several variations on the story of how this came to happen, but I recall that it happened this way:

The great designer Nudie Cohn arrived in the San Fernando Valley from New York where he had manufactured custom-made ladies' foundation garments, primarily for the ladies of burlesque, in the late 1940s. On the weekends, Nudie and his wife, Bobbie, went to Western music halls and Nudie soon began making clothes for some of the Western bands. Eventually he made enough money to open Nudie's Rodeo Tailors at the intersection of Victory Boulevard and Vineland in North Hollywood.

Just as an aside, I always thought the name "Nudie" was in reference to his former occupation. In fact, it is based on his given name, "Nutya." The young man who welcomed him to Ellis Island couldn't spell "Nutya" and so recorded his name as "Nudie" Cohn.

Around this same time, Dad met Nudie at a party and they discovered they had similar ideas about the design of Western clothes. Dad and Mom became two of Nudie's best customers and Dad was so pleased with Nudie's work that he helped finance the shop. This was the start of a lifelong friendship and collaboration.

Dad was always concerned about being seen by the kids high up in the cheap seats of the arenas where they performed. Some of the arenas they played were huge, Madison Square Garden in particular. Just prior to an appearance there, Dad approached Nudie about putting rhinestones on his shirts and down the legs of his pants—this looked great under the spotlights. Dad liked the look of fringe across his shoulders and down his arms when he rode horses. He said that it looked like "fluttering flags" when he made his running entrance on Trigger—and this became one of his signature looks. Then he got what Nudie acknowledged was his best idea, putting rhinestones on the leather fringe. Now when he rode into an arena, the lights would catch the thousands of dancing rhinestones and the night would be filled with millions of little reflected lights.

Dad even devised the distinctive block and shape of his hat. He said that he wanted something that was different, something that no one else had and that would allow him to be easily identified in a crowd. He even came up with a modified version for Mom.

Mom soon joined the design team when she provided her freehand sketches for a new look. She had the idea that their outfits should complement each other and she started coming up with designs that were themed for the event where they were going to appear. Their Washington, D.C., outfits, for instance, were decorated with cherry blossoms—while the outfits designed for Dallas and Houston had longhorns or oil wells. Her designs added the finishing touch to their unique look.

Hats, however, were not Mom's strong suit. She loved hats and wore a lot of them. She believed that hats should complement an outfit but could also be fun and should attract attention to the wearer. She was sure able to do that. Mom's original-design Christmas hat is in the museum and is a white Stetson with angel hair draped around the brim. She placed small, variegated Christmas ornaments in the angel hair, and finished it off with a 10-inch miniature Christmas tree, green with the tips of the branches painted white, atop the crown. She wore this original creation on a television show and to church during the holidays. I won't even try to describe the Easter bonnet that combined an Easter basket and fake eggs. Even though her flights of whimsy were sometimes "over the top," we still joined in her laughter and sense of good fun as she wore her "Dale Originals" every chance she got.

But the one hat that affected me most came about when one of Dad's friends presented him with a pair of 4-inch baby bull's horns. Dad mentioned to Mom that he didn't know what to do with them. Mom thought for a few moments and then asked Dad if she could have them. She called on Nudie to help her with the construction of her latest design. He built, to her specifications, a black-and-white cowhide beanie that tied in a bow under her chin with long thin black leather thongs. Atop the beanie, on either side of center, were the baby bull's horns.

There is a picture in the museum of the family leaving church—and Mom is wearing the Horn Hat! There is another picture in the museum of Mom attired in a very sophisticated black strapless evening gown, the caption under this picture reads, "Savoy Hotel, London," and Mom is wearing the Hat again. But there is no picture of Mom wearing the Hat when she made an appearance as my piano accompanist at an assembly at Canoga Park High School. She had arrived too late to come backstage (not unusual) and I had no idea that she was wearing the Hat until I walked onto the stage and looked down at my accompanist. I wanted to die, or at least have a big hole open up and swallow me.

The only time I remember Dad ever wearing anything remotely out of character was when he decided to play a practical joke on the family. Dad planned to surprise us by wearing a custom-tailored Irish tweed suit, sporting a homburg and carrying a bumbershoot, when we picked him up at LAX. He had purchased this incredible outfit when passing through London on his way home from an African safari and thought it would be a great practical joke to play on us. However, his appearance was so startling that the airline's London staff had alerted their press people in L.A., and the next day's newspaper carried a picture of Dad coming down the steps of the plane, a proper British gentleman.

It's funny how comfortable they were in their Roy and Dale outfits; it's as though they never gave them a second thought. Mom and Dad's friend, actor Rand Brooks, told us about the first time he met Mom and Dad. It was at Pickfair, Mary Pickford's estate in Beverly Hills, at a charity luncheon and everyone else was dressed in Hollywood casual. But not Mom and Dad! No, they showed up in full Western regalia. Rand said that he was impressed by how easily they wore their clothes and how unself-conscious they were. They later became close friends and Rand appeared in a couple of episodes of the *Roy Rogers Show.*

Another example of how easily they wore their Roy and Dale outfits is the first time they met Larry's mom and dad to help plan our wedding. At the time, they were spokespersons for a local savings and loan and had just hosted the grand opening of a new branch. Here came Mom and Dad into this quiet, middle-class neighborhood. They pulled into Mary and Bill's driveway and stepped out of the car dressed like . . . well, like Roy and Dale. In fact, I think Dad still had his guns strapped on. The neighbors could not believe their eyes, but Mom and Dad came in, as relaxed and comfortable as could be. It's interesting how accustomed they were to wearing their show clothes, because those clothes weren't comfortable at all. Dad's shirt alone must have weighed twenty pounds or more and Mom's outfits were just as heavy.

Another time, when we were living in Connecticut, Dad was on the East Coast doing promotions for his Roy Rogers Restaurants. Larry and I picked Dad up at JFK. He had come directly from the opening of a new restaurant and was in his full-up Roy Rogers outfit, fringed shirt, dress pants, and fancy boots—but no guns this time because the FAA has always taken a dim view of wearing guns on an airline flight. This really was quite a sight, since there aren't that many cowboys in New York or Connecticut, as you might guess, and he stood out even more than usual. It was dinnertime when we picked him up and he had not eaten anything since breakfast. All we could think about was where in the Stamford/Greenwich area we could take Roy Rogers for dinner. Luckily, and typical of Dad, he just wanted to get home and have a peanut-butter-and-jelly sandwich.

Actually, that's kind of too bad. It really deprived some Connecticut diners of what would undoubtedly have become a lasting memory.

13

Sidekicks and Bad Guys

When anyone says "sidekick," the first name that comes to mind is George "Gabby" Hayes. He left his mark on that role like no one else. George had started his stage career on the East Coast appearing in vaudeville and on the legitimate stage, primarily in stock companies. He retired from the theater in his forties but was forced to return to work when he lost all his money in the 1929 stock market crash. From what I remember hearing, it was Momma (his wife Dorothy, a former dancer and his wife since they were teenagers) who had the idea of coming to Hollywood to try his luck in movies. With his stage-trained voice and authoritative presence and, given the fact that movie heroes were usually in their twenties or thirties, George was usually cast as the main villain, a role neither he nor his wife was happy about.

But then he found the role of "Gabby," the comic, irascible old coot in countless Westerns—and that's where he found cinematic immortality.

Everyone adored Gabby, on and off the screen. When Mom was honored at the last Golden Boot Awards that she attended, she didn't want to talk about her career in her acceptance speech; she wanted to talk about the most enduring symbol of Hollywood that she could think of—Gabby Hayes.

The story she wanted to share with the audience that night was about catching her first sight of Gabby. She was arriving at the main gate her first morning at Republic. A large Lincoln convertible was waved through the gate and driving this very luxurious car was what appeared to be an old miner. A full growth of beard covered the man's face, and he wore raggedy clothes and a torn and battered hat. As she left the lot that evening, the same Lincoln was going out the gate. Now the driver's beard was trimmed, he was wearing an obviously expensive tweed suit, smoking a pipe, and the disreputable hat was gone. Mom thought to herself, "Now, I've seen Hollywood." That she had. She had also gotten her first glimpse of Gabby Hayes.

I don't remember a time in my childhood that Gabby wasn't a major part of my Republic experience. I absolutely adored him. He was another grandfather—he even let me sit in his lap and comb that wonderful beard (one of my favorite photographs shows me at about four years old doing just that). When visitors came onto the set, Gabby assumed the funny accent he used when in character and he'd walk the stoop-shouldered "Gabby" walk. The moment they left, he would again be ramrod straight and return to using impeccable English in his beautiful stage-trained speaking voice. "Gabby Whittaker" was the character, George Hayes was the man—but I don't remember calling him anything other than Gabby.

The wonderful Margaret Dumont was working with Mom, Dad, and Gabby in *Sunset in El Dorado* (1945). Film buffs will remember Miss Dumont as the perennial foil for the Marx Brothers in many of their best movies. This was the fourth movie that Mom made with Gabby. He had left Dad's films in 1943 to work with Bill Elliott and didn't return until Mom's fifth film, *Lights of Old Santa Fe* (1944). Mom was filming a scene with Miss Dumont and, after the first take, Mom saw Gabby hopping up and down. He motioned Mom over and told her not to let that actress do that to her. Mom didn't have the slightest idea what he was talking about and asked him what he meant. He said, "She's upstaging you!" Mom still didn't understand what he was talking about.

Later, when Gabby had a scene with Miss Dumont, he went over to Mom and said, "Watch this." Mom said she couldn't appreciate everything that those two old pros were doing to each other, but it involved such things as subtly shifting their weight ever so slightly to change the camera angle for the other person, or Gabby would twitch his nose while Miss Dumont was saying her line, or he'd change the rhythm of his line to throw off her timing. One or the other of them might step into the other's key light, casting a shadow on the other's face, or Miss Dumont would fluff her hair while he was delivering a line, drawing the attention to herself. Mom said she never saw anything like it again. Apparently, those two knew every scene-stealing trick there was.

Between ages three and four, whenever I wanted to see Gabby I just went over to the *Red Ryder* set to visit. That is where I first got acquainted with Bobby Blake, who was playing Little Beaver. He was older than me by several years and was a child star. I remember being fascinated with Little Beaver and enjoyed watching Bob change from this nice Italian boy into the young Indian sidekick. But the main attraction on that set was still Gabby. Like Mom, he never seemed to mind me following him around.

Gabby was devoted to his wife, Dorothy (or Momma as he called her). While on the East Coast they co-starred in many stock company productions, yet when they came to California she worked in department stores to support them until he could get established with the studios. She was always the only critic that he listened to. Mom said that whenever the four of them would go to dinner and talk would turn to work, if "Momma" complimented Gabby on something he had done he glowed. But if Momma offered even the smallest bit of criticism he immediately took it to heart.

I was already a wife and mother the last time I saw Gabby. Bill and I were living in Hawaii, and Gabby was staying at the Royal Hawaiian Hotel. Gabby called and invited me to join him for lunch in his suite and told me to "bring your baby along." When we arrived he immediately started making a fuss over Lisa. Even though he was dressed as George, he made several Gabby faces and talked in his Gabby voice; he even let her pull his beard. She was only about six months old at the time but he enchanted her; she cooed, gurgled, and laughed. Then like the perfect baby she certainly wasn't usually, she dropped off to sleep.

Momma had passed away a few years before and Gabby hadn't said anything about someone else joining us, but the table was set for three. He explained that he always had a place set for Momma. They had never had any children and he was devastated by her loss. It was one of the saddest things I've ever seen. I called Mom after I got home and told her about our lunch. She said that he had done the same thing the couple of times that she and Dad had dinner with him. It made me really glad to have Lisa.

Pat Brady, like Tim Spencer and the other Sons of the Pioneers, was always there. He was always part of our lives, first as the funniest member of the Pioneers, then as Dad's sidekick for fairs and rodeos, then as his sidekick on the TV series. Pat and his wife, Fayetta; Shug Fisher and his wife, Peggy; and Lloyd Perryman and his wife, Buddie, were also friends of Mom and Dad's. They hosted rehearsals, put on backyard barbecues and were generally always around. Pat reminded me of the great comedian Danny Kaye in that they both had rubber faces. Pat loved to make really strange faces and throw us kids into fits of laughter. He was also a fine musician. He and Shug would alternate as bass player for the Pioneers. I don't know why it is, but bass players seem to be the comedians.

Pat and Fayetta never had kids so they were prime targets for Mom and Dad's adoption efforts. One or another of them were always telling us kids that, "We found the perfect little boy or girl for Pat and Fayetta on that last tour." I always hoped that they had because they were so great with kids. On one of our summer tours, Fayetta was one of the adults who helped with corralling the younger siblings. I always thought they were the perfect couple—they even had similar hair color and lots of freckles.

When I worked on the *Roy Rogers Show* with Pat in the "Outlaws of Paradise Valley" episode, he was wonderful to me. I was so nervous and self-conscious it would have been so very easy for him to have totally stolen our scene together. Instead, he was very generous. When the batter blew up in our faces, he went out of his way to make jokes to settle me down and put me at ease.

It was my experience that some of the biggest and nastiest of those bushwackin', back-stabbin' sidewinders were usually some of the nicest guys on the lot. Roy Barcroft, the ultimate bad guy, was the biggest softy you ever saw with little kids. At the Hitching Post Theater on Saturday, it was funny how it usually took Dad a good forty-five minutes to figure Barcroft for the bad guy—every kid in the audience knew it was him from his very first scene. But on the set or at our house, he was a very sweet man. Dad often hunted with Barcroft and with Glenn Strange, who played both bad men and monsters. Glenn was a gentle man who genuinely loved kids. By the time I saw him as the monster in *Abbott and Costello Meet Frankenstein* (1948), I was eight years old. Even with the gruesome makeup, I knew it was Glenn—but I got hysterical anyway and had to be taken home early. Linda Lou and our cousin Doug Wilkins were really mad at me. They were only five and six and they loved the movie. I am not a fan of horror pictures, never was, and never will be.

Evelyn Koleman was the one responsible for getting Roy Rogers and family included in every movie and fan magazine published from 1941 to 1956. "Aunt Evelyn" was Dusty's godmother. She worked for Republic until Dad hired her away in 1950 and made her his East Coast public-relations and merchandising representative. I always found her fascinating. She was the *real* New York publicity woman screenwriters wrote about. She represented my idea of what a New York career woman should be: sophisticated, fast-talking, and always in a rush. She could have given the character in *What Makes Sammy Run* a lot of competition. I don't know how she did it, but she kept Dad's name and face in front of the public.

Art Rush was Dad's manager for almost Dad's whole career. Art, by the time he was 25, was the youngest executive at RCA Victor. He produced records for some of the greatest musical artists in the industry: Jose Iturbi, Lawrence Melchior, Arthur Rubenstein, Nelson Eddy, and Jeanette MacDonald. He left RCA to become managing director of Columbia Management of California, a subsidiary of CBS. Then, Art had, as he later explained to Dad, "tired of the corporate rat race and decided to go into business for himself." He was still managing Nelson Eddy and a couple of other big-name performers but "needed a Western singer-actor to make the list complete." Art contacted Dad in 1939, they talked, and Dad agreed to hire the man who helped make him a superstar of the 1940s, '50s and '60s. Dad's experiences with managers up to that point had all been disastrous. So it's hard to imagine that he and Art never had a contract—they had a verbal agreement and a handshake that sealed their management deal from that day in 1939 until Art died. Dad often said that if he had realized at that first meeting what Art was going to mean to his career, he would have given him a hug rather than a handshake.

Art was also managing Mom when she and Dad met at Edwards Air Force Base and he later managed the Sons of the Pioneers for a number of years.

Dad usually called him Arthur and spoke of him as "Mother Rush." Art was a tall man with a long face and perpetual bags under his eyes. We kids thought that he looked rather like a bloodhound. Poor Art, I think of him more as a border collie, always trying to herd us together while this one or that one would try to break away from the group.

There were so many other people that were in and out of our lives—mainly the singers and musicians and their families. At one time or another Dad had worked with almost everyone who wrote or performed the music that came to define the sound that is known worldwide as "Western" music. The Sons of the Pioneers I have already talked about, but Tex Ritter, Stuart and Suzy Hamblen, Jimmie Wakely, Ray Whitley, Tex Williams, Spade Cooley, Wes and Marilyn Tuttle, and Eddie Dean were all people who were in and out of our lives with great frequency when we were kids. We went to their homes; they came to ours. Several of them were Dad's hunting buddies as well.

I don't remember many single events that stand out that much for me. I was a kid and these were the adults in my life. And their kids were the kids I played with whenever our parents got together. I didn't attend school with them, I just played with them; we attended some of the same birthday parties or we would see each other at the studio or an event that our parents had taken us to.

I vaguely recall Candice Bergen being at Dusty's third birthday party. She was there because Mom asked her father, Edgar Bergen, to bring Charlie and Mortimer to the party. Because he and Mom were friends and former co-stars of the Chase and Sanborn show, he did! Looking back on that now it seems unbelievable; he was a huge star, I can't believe that he did that. But he was also Mom's friend and co-worker.

Dad occasionally shot skeet and trap with Clark Gable. I had already seen *Gone With the Wind* (1939) and *Across the Wide Missouri* (1950) and when Dad introduced me to Mr. Gable, I thought I wouldn't be able to breathe. Mr. Gable was not having a good day at the range but he was still very nice to a tongue-tied fourteen-year-old. I think I even said something like, "You're my biggest fan," which was one of those things that people were always saying to Dad that we kids found hysterically funny after they had walked away. Here I was saying it to Mr. Gable who, like Dad, knew what I really meant and was very gracious.

Of course, everyone has heroes. Mom's was Charlton Heston. One night, Mom called me and said, "Oh you won't believe what Dad and I are going to go to! We are going to see Charlton Heston in *A Man for all Seasons*!" This was definitely not my Dad's cup of tea and how she got him to do it I have no idea. I guess he knew she was just crazy about Charlton Heston, so he decided to give in. I told her I was real tickled for her and to let me know how it was.

The next morning, the phone rang early. Usually, if a call came in at around 7:30 A.M. I knew it was Mom. She sounded so excited: "You won't believe what happened! Chuck asked us backstage!" She was as breathless as any teenager who had been summoned by Elvis Presley and just absolutely adorable. Arguably, she was just as famous—maybe even more so—than he was, but Mom was totally starstruck. He was Charlton or Mr. Heston two weeks earlier, and now he was "Chuck." She went on and on about how wonderful his performance was and how gracious he was and she couldn't believe that he asked her backstage. Of course, Mom and Dad got asked backstage all the time by all sorts of stars—but this was special. This was Chuck!

Both Robert Taylor and Dale Robertson had offered to buy a buckskin colt that we had bred at our ranch in Chatsworth and that I considered mine. As everyone knows, they were both matinee-idol handsome and Dale Robertson had one of the best speaking voices in town—I had a crush on both of them and couldn't believe it when they came, at different times, to *my house* to see *my colt*. Dale is a member of the Golden Boot Committee and we occasionally run into each other at Western festivals. Now we laugh about the incredibly gauche young girl who practically drooled whenever she saw him. I think, however, it was a reaction he was used to.

Natalie Wood was a swimming companion for the couple of years we lived in Encino. We didn't attend school together, but we had several mutual friends. She was a lovely teenager and I had always admired her acting ability. As a child she was a huge star but, like so many child actors, she was in the doldrums of her career. In Hollywood, lives can change almost overnight. We were swimming together the summer of 1954 but when I returned from Kemper Hall the summer of 1955, *East of Eden* had already been released and created a sensation, and Natalie was well on her way to becoming a superstar. I never saw her in person again but I thrilled at her success and wept over her tragic death.

14

Adventures with Roy

When Dad traveled, he almost always made the local children's hospital one of his first stops. Mostly, he did it with no fanfare but sometimes the publicity department stepped in and played it up or the local newspapers would get wind of it from someone on the hospital staff and send a reporter. This definitely was not the purpose of his visit and, although he would be courteous to them, he would keep the press as far away as possible from the kids he was there to see.

The effect that he had on really ill kids, and sometimes adults, too, was absolutely amazing. He always asked who the sickest patients were and made it a point to visit with them if possible. He always had a message of encouragement and usually left patients with smiles on their faces, no matter how sick they were.

Sometimes he even brought Trigger to the hospital. Can you imagine anyone taking a horse into a children's hospital today?

Dad also made hundreds of telephone calls all over the world to encourage sick kids and admonish them to "get well for Trigger and me." Sometimes he would extend an invitation to them to visit the "Double R Bar" when they recovered.

But if one of his own kids got sick, it was a different story altogether. He couldn't handle that at all.

When I was sixteen, I became very ill and was admitted to St. Joseph's Hospital in Burbank for ten days while the doctors tried to find out what was wrong. The doctors thought I had appendicitis but after waiting awhile for my appendix to burst, they discovered that I had kidney stones. Mom was there almost every day but even though the hospital was just across the Valley from where we lived, Dad did not come to see me even once. I remember talking to Mom on the telephone and hearing her telling Dad that he had to at least speak to me—which he only did reluctantly. That seems kind of odd and uncaring but I don't believe it was. I just don't think that he could handle the helpless feeling you get when it's your own kid and you can't do anything to fix what's wrong.

Dusty often mentions that he resented having to share Mom and Dad with millions of other kids, but I didn't see it that way. I thought it was neat that other kids admired my parents and wanted to be part of the family. However, at times like that, when I was sick, I could understand what he meant. I am not certain how the others felt, but I always figured that it was just how things were.

How could Dad be just an ordinary father when he was known and recognized around the globe? We have photos of Dad arriving in Nairobi, Kenya, for his first trip to Africa. The photos show thousands of people greeting his plane. We were astonished. Our expectations of Africa were thatched huts and sparsely clad tribesmen, and it never occurred to any of us that they would have theaters or would have seen cowboy movies. But there they were, Roy Rogers fans by the thousands.

Towards the end of his life we had a busload of recent Russian emigrants visit the museum. When Dad learned of this he said, "I've always wondered if any of my movies were ever shown behind the Iron Curtain?" Then he left his office and headed into the museum on Trigger III, the motorized cart he used to get around the museum. The group was about fifty strong and filled the museum lobby. As Dad drove through the lobby they parted like the Red Sea, promptly surrounded him and started applauding. You should have seen their expressions. They couldn't believe that the famous Roy Rogers was actually welcoming them to his museum. They kept asking, "Is Roy Rogers?" When we assured them that he was, they would say, "No! Is really Roy Rogers?"

Dad was as overwhelmed as the Russians!

When you realized that Dad truly was one of the most recognized people of his century, how could you expect him to be just, *Dad*? It was times like that when I was reminded how truly special my father was.

The times I was able to spend with my dad are among some of my greatest memories. Dad was one of my favorite dates. I loved going places with him, mostly because he was so spontaneous.

When Dad was working at Paramount filming *Son of Paleface* (1956) with Bob Hope, the lot was overrun with circus people filming *The Greatest Show on Earth*. Ringling Bros. and Barnum & Bailey circus performers were practicing their skills everywhere there was an unoccupied space. A few months later, Dad and Mom were invited to the movie's world premiere.

I was so excited for them—it was the first premiere I remember them attending. Mom and I had gone shopping for the dress she would wear and she was going to be one of the most beautiful ladies there. A day of so before the premiere Mom got very sick and Dad said he wasn't going without her. Mom suggested that I could be Dad's guest and she supervised the choosing of my dress, how my hair would be done, everything. I was so excited. Dad was going to wear his custom-made tuxedo with the white ruffled shirt and a brocade cummerbund. I was going to wear a long black skirt of Mom's with a beautiful white blouse with ruffles. Mom even loaned me a pearl choker and I would have flowers in my hair. At eleven, I felt I was finally being recognized as the adult I was!

On our big night, we ate an early dinner, then got "all duded up," one of his favorite expressions. We were on our way to Hollywood when Dad spotted his favorite drive-in on the corner of Laurel Canyon and Ventura. My father had the most incredible sweet tooth. He always said that he had a built-in magnet that wouldn't allow him to pass a Foster's Freeze or A&W stand, which was all right with us kids. The car was suddenly drawn into the drive-in and Dad ordered two milkshakes from the carhop. At that time you had your choice of a tray that hung outside the car's window or one that hung from the steering wheel. Dad chose the latter. You guessed it! No sooner had the carhop brought our shakes than Dad sneezed. His knee flew up, hit the tray and our shakes went flying all over both of us. Disaster! If I had been with anybody else, we would probably have immediately turned around and gone home. But Dad just called the carhop over and we made emergency repairs. We almost had to peel in order to get the ice cream off our clothes. Dad began to grin and then to giggle, which was catching.

We arrived at the premiere a rather sodden couple. Dad's ruffled shirt now had limp, damp ruffles. My white ruffled blouse looked as though we had been caught in a rain shower. So much for glamour. But every time we would looked at each other, or noticed someone looking at us with a quizzical expression, we would start giggling again. Dad had managed to turn the whole event into a big joke and I had a wonderful time. When we later told Mom about our adventure, she mumbled something under her breath that sounded a lot like, "Typical!"

Even if the outing was a magazine layout, he was fun to be with. We have a copy of a magazine spread that was shot at a kids' amusement park that used to be on Ventura Boulevard just a few blocks from the studio. Linda Lou and I were really small, probably two and five, and Dad was taking us on all the rides. As I said, this was a park for children, small children, yet there was Dad with us in a bumper car, or in a tethered airplane that went around in circles, having just as much fun as Linda and me. He never really stopped being a kid at heart. I think he always came across the screen that way. I believe that's why a lot of people were charmed by him and drawn to him.

Which reminds me of one of the funniest descriptions I've heard of my dad. When girls would learn who my dad was, they would invariably talk about how much they were in love with him, how handsome he was and how when they grew up, they were going to marry him. Larry and I were in Nashville where our friend Fred Goodwin had us making the rounds, and we stopped by the Country Music Hall of Fame. We were downstairs in the archives visiting with the staff when we were introduced to Buck

Owens's (of *Hee Haw* fame) former wife, Bonnie Owens, a fine performer in her own right. When she learned who I was, she gushed, "Oh, honey, I was so in love with your Dad. . ." Here it comes, I thought. Then she continued, "that I was going to marry him when *he* grew up. But he never did!" That did it, Larry and I were both on the floor doubled over with laughter. Boy! Did Bonnie Owens know my father!

Mom was in St. Joseph's Hospital with pneumonia on my fourteenth birthday. She and Dad had planned a wonderful party for me. I was allowed to invite three girls and four boys and we would go on Dad's converted PT boat, The Flamba, over to Catalina for the weekend. Dad was already taking a group of scuba divers out—they were trying to set a depth record for diving with scuba gear—and photographers who were recording the dives. But Mom got sick and Dad ended up hosting the scuba people and acting as our chaperon. We left San Pedro and headed across the Catalina Channel. Dad was busy with the divers and I am sure that he felt we couldn't get into any trouble mid-channel. I knew better, but I fell asleep on the deck of the boat. By the time we reached the island, my face, back and legs had begun to swell. One of my girlfriends was a very fairskinned strawberry blonde; she had protected her face with a hat but her back and legs were burned as badly as mine were.

I remember being horribly nauseated—happy birthday!—so Dad put my girlfriend and me ashore at the guest ranch and called Mom to see what he should do. From her hospital bed she arranged everything. She snagged a doctor going down the hall and told him of our plight. He said that it sounded as though we had sun poisoning and recommended that Dad bring us back to L.A. as early as possible the next morning. Meanwhile, our burns should be kept as cold as possible; we had both already started running fevers. We had the guest ranch staff bringing us bags of ice throughout the night. I don't remember much of anything of the return trip except that we were miserable.

Poor Dad, he never knew what to do if any of us were in pain and we were a mess. We made it home and got treatment for our burns and that is the last time I ever laid out in the sun—the burn left me with an extreme allergy to the sun. It's been long-sleeved garments, big floppy hats, and zinc oxide for me ever since.

It was only a week later that Mom and Dad were scheduled to be the grand marshals of the Portland Rose Festival in Oregon. Mom was just getting out of the hospital and there was no way she could survive a weekend of public festivities and riding in a parade. So, again I got to take her place!

My face had turned strange shades of purple, it cracked from the sunburn and liquid was oozing from the cracks—I looked like the victim of some mad slasher. Mom told me to slather Panstick makeup on my burns and suggested that rather than cleanse my face each evening (touching my face was agony), that I simply re-touch my makeup each morning with a little more Panstick. And that's what I did.

Poor Dad. Mom is in the hospital and he has this very strange-looking teenager with him. The people of Portland must have thought me terribly "Hollywood." A celebrity's kid whose parents allowed her to wear much too much makeup. But he carried the whole thing off as though there were nothing unusual about my looks—in fact, he acted as if I always looked like that.

Ah, the glamorous life of a celebrity—but I swear that the happenstance of accompanying Dad is what kept my face from being scarred for life by the sunburn. Somehow the Panstick protected my burned skin and by the time we returned home the next week, healing was well underway and there was almost no scarring. The only time people comment is if I get overheated—then my skin gets very blotchy. Being in that parade with Dad turned out to be very beneficial.

15

The Roy Rogers Show

he Roy Rogers Show first hit the air on NBC on December 30, 1951. Set in Mineral City and on the Double R Bar Ranch—where everyone came to assume we lived in real life—the stories took place in the modern-day West. In addition to Mom and Dad—who were, of course, already audience favorites—TV viewers came to know and love other members of the cast, both human and not: Pat Brady as Dad's comic sidekick; those magnificent horses, Trigger and Buttermilk; the brave German Shepherd, Bullet; and, of course, Pat's famous Jeep, Nellybelle. The show was in production until 1957, but ran in worldwide syndication for years afterward.

I think the transition to television was a very easy one for Mom and Dad to make.

Dad had hired so many of his old Republic crew, stuntmen, and character actors, it was as if we were still at the Republic lot in Studio City even though we were now filming at Samuel Goldwyn Studios in Hollywood.

They were used to working fast and furious at Republic, and that turned out to be perfect training for TV. At Republic, known for its action-packed, fast-paced serials, they would turn out as many as 40 setups in a day. Given that, it wasn't much of a stretch for the crew to switch over to the similar demands of TV production, and of course that's one of the reasons Dad wanted them.

They produced four episodes every ten working days. You would cast the same guest stars and the same bad guys in two episodes—simply changing a vest and hat, and the character's name. That way, they could film two episodes at a time. The shows would air several months apart, so the viewers didn't really notice. But in those days, that was how you stretched the budget to film a series like *The Roy Rogers Show* and make it economically feasible. Those were also the days before the unions were so powerful. Television crews worked six days, often from daybreak until 11:00 at night. Most of the exteriors for Dad's shows were filmed at famous Iverson's Ranch, which was just behind our ranch in Chatsworth. Since about 1914, Iverson's has served as the distinctive backdrop of hundreds of movies and TV shows that ranged from sci-fi to Westerns. Then, as *The Roy Rogers Show* was winding down, Dad began producing *Brave Eagle,* and many of the exterior shots for that series were taken in our front yard in Chatsworth. The boys from the Canoga Park High School football team came over and raced canoes in the big lake that had been built in our front yard for that series.

I was always fascinated with all the action on the set, and I became involved in the show to a very small extent. During the last season, they even shot some of *The Roy Rogers Show* episodes at our house in Chatsworth. Even when they were shooting over at Iverson's, I would beg to come along. I think I liked to go more than the other kids; I loved being around all that action. I don't remember Linda ever being more than mildly interested with being on the set. And Dusty seemed mainly bored with it; he wouldn't be quiet so people were always hollering at him to shut up. I had been trained to be quiet since I was two or three years old, so I was familiar with the discipline of filming.

Once we moved to Chatsworth, Iverson's was practically next door. Mimi had arrived from Scotland to join the family and there was now someone interested in going with me to Iverson's. I got my driver's license shortly before the show completed its run. After school and on weekends, I would take my friends "on location" to see how films were made.

We would drive up there in my 1950 Chevy tank, Gertrude the Gutless Wonder.

I had earned the money for my car, but Dad chose her. His daughter had to have a car that was safe. And, *safe* is exactly what Gertrude the Gutless Wonder was. She was that awful standard hospital green that Chevy used in 1950–51. She was a three-speed stick-shift and had earned her nickname "Gutless." But she was *definitely* safe. I think she would have survived a fall off a cliff and not received more than a slight dent. Of course, she would vapor lock on Iverson's dirt roads during hot weather. I remember more than one chase scene having to be postponed so that Gertrude could be pushed out of the way.

Mimi and I, along with several of our girlfriends, would hang out on the set whenever we could and came up with nicknames for some of the cast and crew. Rand Brooks was "The Juvenile." We just adored him—and who wouldn't? Rand worked in any number of TV shows in those days and was in many, many films. But audiences today probably best remember him as Scarlett O'Hara's first husband in *Gone With the Wind*. He's a terrific actor but an even better human being. Then and now he is an absolute love and one of my favorite people.

Linda Lou and I nicknamed Stuart Whitman "Handsome" when he guest-starred in a couple of the early episodes. He was just getting started in his acting career and we thought him the essence of what a young leading man should look like. He was newly wed to a beautiful, tall, red-headed model. We thought them the most romantic couple and didn't allow them a moment of privacy for his five days on the set.

There was a very handsome older "heavy" that we named "Doggie." Neither Linda nor I can remember why. It certainly had nothing to do with his looks. He was slender, played the crooked banker or rancher, was well-coifed with his grey-streaked pompadour. He worked on several of the episodes and was always "Doggie."

Then there was "Jesus." Bill Catching was a great stuntman. He had joined the TV series to be Dad's stunt-double, then he became the series' stunt coordinator (that's the guy who designs and directs the stunts) in addition to doing stunts himself. We had this beautiful picture in our dining room of Jesus with his arms outstretched and little children surrounding Him. My kid sister Dodie always thought that Bill looked liked that particular picture of Jesus. Whenever Bill came up to the house or she'd see him somewhere else, Dodie would always say, "Look Mom, there's Jesus!" We always teased her and him, and still do because he is still a very good friend that we see quite often.

Producing a TV series was often grueling work, but there was plenty of time for fun—or mischief—too. Dad was very competitive and loved any kind of game. Of course, there were card games going on all the time between setups. They never played for any real money—never more than maybe a quarter a point, and more often they'd just play for matchsticks. But even so, Mom didn't approve of gambling. Bill Catching loves to tell the story of the day that a group of the guys were playing cards for money, with their quarter limit. Dad was facing the house and the other people had their backs toward the house. All of a sudden, he stood up and turned over the table; the cards, nickels, and dimes went flying. Dad yelled, apparently furious, "I told you guys there was no gambling on this set!" and he stormed away . . . just as Mom rounded the corner. I doubt that she was fooled.

Mom was pretty much in charge of the morals on the show. She placed a "cuss box" on the set from the very beginning. She hadn't done that at Republic, but as soon as it was their own company she did. I think they had to put in a quarter every time they swore. All the money collected in the cuss box went to the church. It was amazing how much money she collected for "good works" during the first couple of weeks, but it's also amazing how quickly the crew became aware of what they were saying, and the set soon became a more refined place for her small children to hang out.

When I was little, maybe eight or nine, I gave Dad a story line for one of the radio shows—and they actually used it! I remember being thrilled that they used my idea. But darned if I can remember what the idea was. It seems to me it featured Dad and a little girl but that's the extent and sum total of plumbing my memory.

Mom saw to it that we got to film commercials. She insisted that we be paid, but we never saw the money, because it was put away for us—that's what bought Gertrude the Gutless Wonder. Those monies went straight into savings accounts, with our names on them, to be used when we really needed it. Mom was financially very conservative and tried to instill the same values in us. In other words, she wanted us to develop the habit of saving for a rainy day. Some of the commercials we did were for Sugar Crisp, Nestle, Post Cereals, and products for cookies, salad dressing, and others that have slipped into the memory gap. Those were real family affairs: Mom, Dad, and all the kids. Later commercials included some of the grandchildren, too.

I began my career in theatrical films at the age of ten when Dad was filming a movie called *Trail of Robin Hood* (1950). It was a movie meant to be released during the holiday season and the storyline was about Christmas tree thieves. Republic was using most of the cowboy heroes they had under contract at the time: Allan "Rocky" Lane, Rex Allen, Monte Hale, Ray Corrigan, Kermit Maynard, and Tom Keene. There was a scene in the film where a bunch of kids are at a turkey shoot. I am the little girl that asks Jack Holt for his autograph. Billy Witney was the director. Mom coached me on "my line" the night before and we got the scene after just two rehearsals and three takes, and I wasn't the one responsible for the retakes. I was on cloud nine. I was in a movie! I was an actress!

I was probably obnoxious for weeks!!!

When I was fifteen, I got a chance to appear in one of the TV episodes. Now, I had been lobbying for this ever since I had made my screen debut in *Trail of Robin Hood*. After all, I had said my line without fault and I had been sure for a long time that I was ready for a more challenging part.

In my scene, Pat Brady was supposed to teach me how to make pancakes; he was the cook at the show's Mineral City Café. The indoor set at Goldwyn's had a whole professional restaurant setup with a large griddle like you might see in a fast-food restaurant. Well, somebody came up with the idea that since Pat was the comedian, it would be really funny that if every time Pat put batter on the griddle, it would give off clouds of smoke. The only trouble was, they couldn't get the batter to smoke; so they loaded it up with everything they could think of. Nothing worked. Finally, some genius got the bright idea to put kerosene in it.

Yes, that's right, kerosene. Over an open flame!

They were shooting a close-up of Pat and me, and had us both practically right over the griddle. When Pat ladled on that special kerosene-laced batter, there was a big whoosh; it ignited and blew up in our faces. The explosion took all my eyebrows and my eyelashes off, and partially ignited my bangs. Pat's arm was singed. Everybody was running all over the place; it caused a big to-do—but I sure got a lot of attention! Even today when I see the director Les Martinson, I remind him of the day he tried to kill me!

If you want to see the episode it's called "Outlaws of Paradise Valley." Of course, you won't see the explosion, and you'll notice that the batter doesn't smoke either. I think they decided there had been enough excitement for one day and decided to play the scene the way it had originally been written—without the gag.

I was really too inhibited to be a good actor. I liked the idea of it, but I couldn't get comfortable in front of a camera. However, I did love to sing and with Mom and Dad's coaching, became reasonably good at it. In 1956, the Frontiersmen were appearing at a club out in Newhall. It was a country-western music hall where people gathered on weekends to listen to good music and get in some dancing. Dad had been friends with Hi Busse, the leader of the Frontiersmen, since his old radio days and I had known Hi all of my life. On Saturday nights, the management allowed for a couple of open-mike sessions and for several weeks Hi had been encouraging me to step up and do a couple of numbers. I finally got up my nerve one Saturday when it seemed as though all of my friends were out of town.

I stepped up to the mike and sang one of my favorite songs, *The Yellow Rose of Texas*. Well, the ceiling didn't fall in on me and the audience actually seemed to enjoy my song. Hi continued to encourage me and I joined the Frontiersmen every Saturday night I was in town.

About a year later, I was singing with a small group of musicians at a holiday event in Chatsworth. I had received a call earlier in the week from a man saying he worked for the *Ed Sullivan*

Show in New York and asking if I would be singing anyplace in the area during the following two weeks. I told him about the gig in Chatsworth and he said that I should look for him there. I told Mom that someone was playing a joke on me, and then didn't think any more about it.

Sure enough, when we were taking a break between sets, a gentleman came up to me and introduced himself, reminding me of our telephone conversation. He said that he had enjoyed the set we had just finished and that I could expect to hear from him again. When I returned home that evening, I told Mom that I really thought this was going a little far for a joke, and Mom agreed. Sure enough though, I heard from the gentleman again. Only this time he was offering me a chance to be on the *Ed Sullivan Show*!

I never did find out if Mom or Dad set it up. I only know that I was sure that I hadn't done anything myself to merit such a chance and it scared me to death. I was also engaged at the time. I told my fiancé what had happened and he was adamant that I turn the offer down. He never went to hear me sing and somehow felt very threatened by my performances. Being the young, scared teenager that I was, I listened to my fiancé and turned down an appearance on the *Ed Sullivan Show*! What an idiot!

But looking at what Mom and Dad went through, the demands on their time, no private life (in fact, hardly any life at all sometimes), I was just never willing to make the sacrifices necessary to be in the limelight. There is plenty of glamour and attendant glitter, but most don't know about the price you pay for that glamour. At our house, we saw living examples of that cost, every day.

16

The Irresistible Force
and the Immovable Object

om and Dad worked in what we'd today call "nontraditional jobs." Because of their unusual work schedule, it was always necessary for our family to have live-in domestic help. Boy, did we have some characters! The interesting thing was that most of them had no previous work experience outside their own homes.

Mom tended to be very humanitarian in her hiring and often selected them pretty much on the basis of her perception of their need. Sometimes they were in financial straits, sometimes they were widows who just needed something to do, and sometimes they were just "Mom's poor souls," the kind of people Mom wanted to help.

She possessed great understanding and warmth and people were really drawn to her; they would pour out their life histories and all of their problems. As much as people were drawn to her, Mom was truly drawn to helping them. She was always just as happy to help strangers solve their problems, as she was to offer advice and moral support to her own friends and family.

If they worked at the house, they were given full reign to discipline us kids, and this led to some interesting confrontations. Most of the ladies were very nice, but a couple, it seemed to me, had been soured by their life circumstances. They tended to take out their bitterness on us when Mom and Dad weren't around. Again, I took my position of "being responsible for the little ones" very seriously and was resentful—and often confrontational—if I thought they were being unfair to my younger siblings.

Because Dusty was "Roy Jr.," he received very little discipline from anyone other than Mom or Dad. But a couple of the ladies who worked for us thought that they could get away with picking on Mimi, Sandy, and Debbie, and I saw it as my job to let them know that their actions would be reported to Mom upon her return. It was probably a good thing that I was almost always either at school or working and hardly ever at home.

And rarely could they cook. I've had stomach problems for most of my life, but after the "food" we were served by some of these women over the years, I wonder that we *all* didn't suffer from stomach problems. There was one of the housekeepers, during the time that Quaker Oats was Mom and Dad's sponsor, who could consistently serve up virtually inedible oatmeal—every morning. And since this was Dad's sponsor, we had cases of oatmeal in the garage. We were really excited when Post Cereals became a sponsor—at least that was cold cereal and not subject to much error in preparation. We also had cases of Nestle Quik and Lux soap, since Mom had appeared on the Lux radio show and on *Lux Video Theater*.

But just because Mom needed some help in running the household doesn't mean that she didn't give everything she had toward being a great mother. And believe me, she really tried her hardest. My Mom was a very gifted and creative woman. In some aspects of her life she was simply brilliant. And in other aspects, well. . . .

Remember that she was married at fourteen, a mother at fifteen, divorced at sixteen, and a single, working mother that same year. It's no wonder that she never had a chance to pick up all that many housewife/homemaker skills along the way. But when she married Dad and was suddenly presented with an instant family, she tackled it like everything else in her life and expected to master it. She often said that Dad went after everything "as though he was killing snakes." In return, Dad said that Mom would do whatever task she had set for herself, "even if it hare-lipped every cow in Texas." I never quite understood that one. The point is, they both did things full-steam ahead, giving them all the effort and stamina that it took to get the job done.

But just because Mom did things full-tilt, didn't mean that she did them right.

In the '40s, they bought Noah Beery Jr.'s old house in Hollywood, where Vine ends and becomes Ivarene on the bend. It was a big, wonderful house and you could see it from all over. Well, you could *really* see the house from all over after Mom got her hands on it, because she painted it barn red with battleship grey trim! And yes, it looked just as hideous as it sounds. It was a three-story house with a crenellated roof and you could see it forever. None of us kids wanted to admit that we lived there because it was so ugly. It had been really pretty when they bought it.

Because Mommy (Arline) had been acknowledged as an exceptional cook and homemaker, poor Mom (Dale) decided that she was going to be just as perfect. For her, nothing but her best was ever acceptable. She once made matching outfits for Linda Lou and me. Mom sewed them by hand because she didn't know how to work the sewing machine. By the time she got our dresses finished, they were up to our knees or slightly above and we could hardly fit our shoulders in them—we had grown so much from when she started.

She had been a career woman since she was fifteen and became a single mother. She married her childhood sweetheart. He liked having a playmate but he really didn't want a family, and they were both too young to realize the difference; he was nineteen and she was fourteen. He didn't like the pregnancy. He didn't like having a baby. He was in and out of her life for about three years and my grandparents finally put their foot down and said to Mom, "You are a parent and this can't keep happening!" They forced her into making a decision that she hadn't wanted to make because she was wild about him. But he was just very irresponsible. And so she divorced him.

She really never did learn to cook—and then she married Dad who was a hunter. Mom didn't really approve of hunting. But she was a great one for taking vows and making promises. So she vowed when they got married that she would cook everything he killed. The result of that particular vow was some of the most, well, "interesting" meals ever. And by "interesting," I mean "inedible." But she really tried. When my kids were growing up, they always wanted to know who was cooking when we went to the folks' for the holidays. They would pray it was potluck. They would say, "If Grandma is cooking, we are eating before we go."

Mom really tried, and she wanted to be the perfect Mom. With Tommy she couldn't afford good food, she couldn't afford good shoes for him when he was a kid growing up. So she made sure that Linda Lou, Dusty, and I had all of the advantages that she wasn't able to give Tommy.

Alfalfa Switzer from the *Our Gang* comedies was a friend of Dad's. Dad sort of adopted him as a kid growing up and they hunted together. As I mentioned earlier, Mom had sworn that whatever Dad hunted she was going to cook. Alfie and Dad were both awful practical jokesters; they pulled just terrible stunts on each other. Alfie's jokes often had a cruel edge to them—he was a pretty messed-up kid. One time he knew that my brother Tom and his wife, Barbara, were coming for dinner. Tom has the weakest stomach in the world even to this day. I think they were newly-weds and this was one of the first times that Mom had invited them for dinner. Dad had recently killed a bear and Alfie was the one who skinned it and prepared it, cutting it into roasts and whatever else had to be done.

Mom had slaved in the kitchen all day and had prepared the potatoes and gravy. The roast looked really pretty and Dad cut and served pieces—and Tommy's piece still had some hair on it. Well, *that* dinner was over that very minute.

Dad always talked about how wonderfully his mother cooked possum back in Ohio. Mom was determined that she was going to make it like Mammy Slye had. Now, the trick with possum is that you are supposed to leave some of the fat on because it's an extremely lean, dry meat. Alfie cut all of the fat off. As usual, Mom waited to try this experimental dish when there was going to be company—she was always doing things like that—and the cooked possum looked sort of like an alley cat when it came out of the oven. It was just pitiful, really pitiful.

Mom could turn even the most ordinary event into a strange adventure. Soon after Mimi came to live with us, she accompanied us on a trip to Mexico. Every summer Mom would go down to Tijuana and buy perfume and huaraches, hand-tooled leather sandals. There were two or three shops that she just loved and which she'd been dealing with forever. Mom loved to go down there and bargain. Now, being raised in California we siblings found this excruciatingly embarrassing. To us, you pay the price on the tag, you don't bargain. But we loved taking the trip with Mom anyway. This time, the group was me, Mom, Linda Lou, Mimi, and one of our girlfriends.

We were already in San Diego because Dad was racing boats, so we decided to drive across the border to Tijuana. We had a lovely time. Everybody got sandals which were so uncomfortable that nobody ever wore them, other than Mom. And Mom bought her favorite, Joy perfume, because she refused to pay the price in California.

Late in the afternoon, we were in the car waiting to cross the border back into the U.S. and all of a sudden Mom started to panic. She cried, "Mimi, Mimi, you won't be able to get in!" Mimi was here on a student visa and we didn't have her papers with us. Mom was absolutely panic-stricken. She got hysterical and so naturally we *all* got hysterical. Mom was trying to figure out how in the world to smuggle Mimi back into California. She was absolutely certain that they would take one look at Mimi and arrest her—and probably all of us. Mom just "knew" Mimi was going to get left in Mexico at the border—and then she would be sent back to Scotland and we'd never see her again

Finally, when we were about two cars from the border, Mom came up with the solution. "Marian," she said, "with that accent they'll know you are not from California. Tell them you are from Texas!"

Well, that broke us all up—even Mom. By the time we got to the border guards we were laughing hysterically and they looked at all these howling kids in the car and they weren't going to keep us down there. They never asked anybody anything.

Nevertheless, she was a wonderful, incredible person. She would meet people in an airplane and talk to them for an hour, and fifteen years later she would meet them and they would say something like, "I was on such-and-such flight with you," and she would reply, "Oh yes and how is that sick baby that you had?" or "How did your wife do with her operation?" She really loved people and she cared and she remembered, and I have never met anybody who was like her.

Dad's public image was as a low-key, laid-back cowboy. Well, he wasn't laid back at home; he was very antsy. He didn't like to sit still at all. He wasn't a reader. He liked music and he liked the outdoors. He was a real physical person. Mom always said that he had been born 100 to 150 years too late because he would have been another Kit Carson, one of the scouts heading West. He just sort of had that bent. He wasn't wild about city life. As 'civilization,' as Dad called it, would catch up to us we would move farther out. We were in Studio City and then, because of Mom, when they first married we were in Hollywood for three years. Then we went to Encino and then Mom and Dad went to Chatsworth. Then when they got most of us raised they ended up going all the way out to Apple Valley where there was *nobody*. There wasn't anybody for a long time out there, and he really liked that.

Mom, even though she was brought up in a small town, was a city girl. Mom would have gone to the theater or to a movie every night if she could. She read everything she could get her hands on—magazines, biographies, history, just anything and everything; she had eclectic taste. Dad just wanted to be off with the dogs.

Whenever a problem would arise in the household, if we were changing housekeepers or if there was a problem with us kids, Dad would take off and go hunting in Mexico or Alaska or Africa, and Mom would get a wire asking, "How are things?" If she said everything was fine, he would come home. If she mentioned there was still a continuing problem he would extend his trip.

Dad didn't like being the bad guy. He really wasn't a disciplinarian; if pushed into it he could become that. My little brothers pushed him into that quite often, but that wasn't what he liked. I think a lot of that was because that wasn't his experience with Grampy. When Dad was a kid, Grampy only came home every other weekend. Since he saw Daddy and my aunts so seldom, I think he was reluctant to be the disciplinarian, and left that sort of thing to my grandmother. So that's the model that Dad grew up with. Dad wanted to be a buddy.

Because our parents—mostly Mom—made us so accountable, we didn't get into that much trouble. But we sure could cause plenty of trouble around the house. And Mom could always give as good as she got.

Even when they were little kids, Sandy always teased Dusty. Dusty had a really short fuse and Sandy knew it, and loved to tweak him whenever he could. We had a big built-in breakfast nook. Most of us would fit on the built-in bench section and there were three seats on the outside and Sandy happened to be on the outside this time, thank heavens. We had a milk cow, and milk was always in a metal pitcher on the table. Sandy had started in on Dusty and Dusty was absolutely furious. He was shouting and hollering and Sandy was goading him and Mom told the boys to stop. She said, "Sandy, don't tease your brother." Well, Sandy didn't stop, so Mom picked up the pitcher of milk and just poured it over Sandy's head.

Sandy was stunned. Everything got quiet at first and then Sandy started to cry. He sounded like Joe E. Brown with that big mouth and that holler that sounded like a siren. The rest of us were just dissolved into laughter—we couldn't believe she had done it.

Later, when Dusty and Sandy were teenagers, they were wrestling in the living room. Dad wasn't making them stop. In fact, he was watching them and laughing. Mom kept yelling, "Boys, stop right now!" But they didn't stop. Mom yelled again. The wrestling continued.

They kept it up until they jostled a lamp and Mom was just sure something was going to get broken. She went down the hallway into her closet and pulled out her gun, the one that she used on the television show. She stepped back into the living room and shouted at the top of her lungs, "BOYS, STOP RIGHT NOW!" There was still no response.

The next thing they heard was BLAM! BLAM! BLAM! BLAM! BLAM! BLAM!

Her gun was loaded with blanks and she fired off all six rounds. The boys fell back, absolutely stunned, afraid they had finally pushed her too far and she had flipped out. Mom later said that even Dad stopped laughing, until he realized what she had done.

Mom was interested in everything. Dad was less obvious in his interests, other than when it came to his dogs, hunting, competitive shooting, and music. As I learned from talking with his closest friends, Dad had a lot more depth and dimension than what he let most people see, including the family.

Mom read everything she could get her hands on, but Dad read mostly scripts or magazines about the outdoors. Mom was a taskmaster as far as our homework went Dad only wanted to know that it was done.

Their differences manifested themselves right from the beginning. Right after they were married, and while Mom was under suspension from the studio, she had a lot of time on her hands so she decided to fix her first fancy meal as a bride. Practically the entire day was spent in preparation for a romantic dinner. Even though we had a cook, she wanted to do the whole thing herself. So she cooked this wonderful meal, went out and bought bouquets of fresh flowers, set the table with the china, crystal, and silverware they had received as wedding gifts, and waited for Dad to come home from work. When Dad walked in the door, Mom called out, "Oh, honey, just a minute, don't come in yet." He waited impatiently in the kitchen while she made the last-minute adjustments in the dining room. She turned the lights off, lit the candles, and told Linda Lou and me to be very quiet. We had already been fed but we had begged to stay up to see Dad's reaction to what she had done. We were allowed to watch from the stairs and thought it all so romantic.

Mom asked Dad to close his eyes, then led him into the dining room where she excitedly told Dad he could open his eyes. Everything was just breathtaking—it looked so pretty that even *I* thought it was wonderful—and I was still mad at her about the marriage! Dad took one look and immediately went over and flipped on the lights. He said that *he* wasn't going to eat anything he couldn't see! This declaration certainly changed the tone of the evening.

He was a real romantic in some ways but not in others. He would shop for her and find beautiful things; he had excellent taste. Mom said that she had always wanted a grandfather's clock, so that's what Dad found for their first anniversary. Every time Dad would go to New York he'd bring back gifts that were absolutely beautiful, incredible pieces of jewelry—which she would promptly misplace—and beautiful gowns and peignoirs.

Dad wasn't a true collector but an "acquirer" of virtually everything. He never got rid of anything, and that is why we have a museum today. However, material things never really meant much to Mom. She gave away everything because she valued things differently. Everything, to her, had to have a purpose and once that purpose had been fulfilled, it would be given or thrown away. "Things" were not important to her—people were. Mom would go through our things saying, "You are much too old for this—your little sisters will enjoy it." The problem was that in my case, "this" would be something such as a set of Disney porcelains which my little sisters immediately broke and which, if I had them today, would probably help put my grandchildren through college.

After they moved to the high desert, Mom, on one of her housecleaning expeditions, threw away the registration papers for two of Dad's thoroughbreds. What Dad had to endure to rectify that, you wouldn't believe. When Dad asked why she had thrown out something so important, she told him that he shouldn't have left them lying on the pool table. Another time, someone called from the dump to tell Dad he had just retrieved a number of government bonds with their names on them. For that one, she had no explanation.

My husband, Larry, has always characterized Mom and Dad's relationship as "the immovable object and the irresistible force," and that pretty much hits the nail on the head. For those people who believe in astrological signs, they were both Scorpios—their birthdays were only five days apart, although he was a year older. Their backgrounds were very different yet similar—and so were their personalities.

Mom would bawl through *An Affair to Remember* again and again and again. Dad liked the bean scene from *Blazing Saddles*— he thought that was one of the funniest things he'd ever seen on screen. Mom was highly insulted by *Blazing Saddles* because the hero rode a palomino and she was upset on Dad's behalf because she thought it was a parody of him. But Dad thought it was absolutely hysterical and he loved it.

I don't remember ever seeing or hearing Mom and Dad fight. I know they did because Mom later told me they had some doozies. But they never fought around us kids.

Mom had not a great sense of humor, but a great *appreciation* of humor. I think one of the things that kept them together is that she thought Dad was the funniest man ever. He was a dreadful tease and she always rose to the bait, and sometimes Mom would be so mad at Dad for something—and out of nowhere he would pull one of his famous one-liners or do something silly to break her up. He would have her in hysterics in no time flat, laughing so hard that she would be fighting for breath and have tears running down her cheeks. Most of their disagreements ended up in laughter. I really believe that that was the secret to their fifty years of marriage. When they first got married they made each other the promise that they would never go to bed angry or without a goodnight kiss. I think they pretty well managed to hold to that.

Mom and Dad might have had some eccentricities, but they were among the most disciplined and professional people I ever met. I don't ever remember hearing of a time that either one of them went to work without being absolutely prepared. They would stay up late at night, or get up even before 4 A.M. to study lines. Mom was just on time for business appointments and Dad was always there an hour earlier than he needed to be—but he was that way all the time, in his personal life, with his friends, and even on hunting trips.

Even though Dad had great natural athletic ability, he was a perfectionist and was never satisfied with his performance. No one will ever know the number of hours he put into perfecting those beautiful mounts you see on the TV series. He would have done his own mounts in the movies as well, but the studio usually wouldn't let him.

I always teased Mom that she didn't like bowling or golf because she couldn't master them. However, this book has made me reexamine some of my long-held beliefs and I now see that she didn't master them because they weren't important to her. Mom preferred parlor games and more genteel activities. Luckily Dad enjoyed these, too. They could play a mean game of cards and they both loved word games. Mom and Dad had a group from their church that met twice a month for years. They had potluck dinners and played parlor games well into the evening.

Mom loved people and she joined us at several Western festivals where Larry and I had a booth for the museum. She really enjoyed meeting and talking to people as she signed her books and participated in panel discussions. Dad, on the other hand, was much more private in nature and was uncomfortable being asked personal questions.

Even though Dad was a natural musician, he never seemed entirely comfortable in front of a live audience. He would often almost get paralyzed with fright before stepping out onto the stage. It was one of the reasons, I think, that he liked doing rodeos and other events in huge arenas—because the audience would blur out and it was easier for him to perform under those circumstances. I was always extroverted and so was Mom—and that's an understatement! She was absolutely the opposite of Dad. Whereas she couldn't wait to get out on stage, he genuinely suffered from stage fright, to the point of physical discomfort. When I was about eleven or twelve, I finally asked him why he put himself through such an ordeal. I remember he answered that it was just part of his job. Mom later said that with some performers, the physical discomfort they suffered seemed to sharpen their performance.

She was certainly right, at least when it came to Dad. Once he was out on that stage, his music took over.

The night I asked Dad that question, he and Mom were performing at a big benefit at the Shrine Auditorium in Los Angeles. This benefit featured a whole line-up of superstars—in fact, it featured the first live performance of Dean Martin and Jerry Lewis on the West Coast. No one wanted to follow their act, but Dad volunteered to close the show, saying that he and Mom were so different from the new comic sensations, that he didn't mind following them. It seemed to me that he was just putting additional pressure on himself. Martin and Lewis came on stage and the audience went wild—they were brought back for two encores. Mom was like a race horse in the starting gate and Dad was nervously pacing back and forth with his hands jammed into his pockets. Martin and Lewis finally left the stage and it was time for Mom and Dad. He was always introduced first and sang a solo number. The announcer could barely be heard above the applause for Martin and Lewis but as soon as Dad stepped out onto the stage, you could tell the applause was for him. By the time Mom and Dad left the stage, the audience had brought them back for two encores and was still clamoring for more. What a night!

That was an incredible evening; Mom let me get all dressed up. I even got to have my hair done in an upsweep fashion and Mom loaned me a lace blouse and floor-length skirt. Boy, did I feel special and all grown-up. I remember Mom introducing me to Tony Martin—Mom had worked with Tony in Chicago during her big band days—and his beautiful wife, Cyd Charisse. I was thrilled to meet the man whose records I played over and over, and she was one of my favorite dancers. I had lots of pictures of both of them in my scrapbooks.

Then Dad introduced me to one of my absolute favorite movie stars, the beautiful Lana Turner, who was even lovelier in person than on the screen. I remember telling Mom afterwards that Miss Turner reminded me of a delicate doll that should have been in a protective glass case.

When Dad introduced us, he said, "Lana. You remember my daughter, Cheryl. You named your daughter after her." I was floored! Typical of Dad, he hadn't said anything about even knowing Miss Turner, let alone saying that she had named her own daughter after me. Wow!

But you know what I remember the most from meeting Lana Turner? She was even more nervous than Dad. Of course, she was a movie actress and didn't usually perform on stage. That evening her only job was to present an award to the head of the Children's Hospital. But I have never seen a performer so nervous either before or since. She was physically sick backstage. Here she was, so beautiful in a white tulle strapless dress, perfectly done hair and makeup, yet she was pacing like a caged animal and with the shakes so bad that it seemed as though she couldn't possibly make it onto the stage.

Then, Mom proved to be right, as usual. When Miss Turner was introduced, she walked onto that stage like the professional she was, said her lines flawlessly, and everyone was enchanted.

Dad was willing to put up with his pre-performance discomfort because his music was so important to him. Years later, Dad told my husband Larry, very matter-of-factly and without boast that he thought he could have been successful at whatever he put his mind to. I think he was right. Anytime he set his mind to a task, he invariably accomplished it.

They were both from farm families, but Dad had grown up dirt poor on the Ohio/Kentucky border. Grampy couldn't make enough money farming to support the family so he took a factory job in town while Mammy ran the small farm. Dad only saw him twice a month. Mom was raised by college educated Southerners whose families had owned plantations. She was even raised by the same black nanny that had raised her Daddy. Mom's parents ran cotton farms that her Mom had inherited.

Dad didn't quite graduate from high school before family finances forced him to look for work. He and his family had nothing before the Depression, even less during its height, and there were no prospects for anything better. That's why Dad and Grampy decided to head out to California—that and the fact that Dad absolutely hated cold weather. Mom, on the other hand, graduated way too early, got married, was divorced, and had to support herself and Tom when she was only sixteen, so Grandma paid for her to go to secretarial school.

Dad's ambition for his kids was that we would earn high school diplomas. To him, that would give you what you needed to be successful. Mom's advice to her daughters was to be sure and take secretarial courses because you needed to prepare for the worst. A woman just couldn't be sure that she wouldn't be widowed or divorced, and we should have a skill to fall back on. After all, it was her secretarial skills that kept her and Tom afloat. The only one of us who got a college degree was Tom. I can't imagine that Mom was ever anything but supportive of his ambitions, but I think it was probably Grandma and Grandfather Smith who set Tom's feet towards the university. In our household, there never was any talk of our going to college; the thrust was always to learn a trade.

Mom was, to me, the most interesting of contradictions. She was a woman who had been earning her own keep since she was sixteen. She became a successful songwriter, actress, singer, author, and motivational speaker and yet she thought that the downfall of modern woman and the American Family was the "women's lib" movement. She and I used to get into some heated discussion about "woman's place." Even though she was a successful, independent woman—boy, was she independent!—she thought that women were meant to be married and should stay home and raise children. Otherwise, we would face divine retribution.

I think that her independence and self-reliance were two of the traits that intrigued Dad. I doubt if he had ever met anybody as strong and opinionated as she. We have some dear friends, Jim and Beverly Rogers, who have meant a great deal to the museum, our family and, especially, Mom in her later years. Jim is a dynamic, successful businessman who has a tongue-in-cheek business card that he passes out to friends. It includes the phrase, "Sometimes wrong but never in doubt." The minute I saw that, I thought it should be transcribed into Latin and incorporated into a coat of arms for Mom. There is no better summation of her personality.

While Mom wouldn't hesitate to give advice to total strangers or close friends, she always seemed to hesitate a bit when it came to giving me advice. I know that she was determined to not be the type of controlling mother that Nana and even her own mother had been. As much as she loved Grandma Smith, Mom often told me that she wouldn't have left Tom's father if Grandma Smith hadn't forced her to. Of course, Mom always seemed to forget that he had left her several times before Grandma stepped in to protect her grandson. Mom seemed to go out of her way to encourage me to make my own decisions, remembering what it was like for her.

Mom and Dad were married more than fifty years. It wasn't a first marriage for either of them, but they shared everything they could and ignored their differences. They adored each other. She was devastated when he died. But here's the difference in their makeup—she lived three years after he passed away. I don't think he would have lived three weeks without her. Nearly every time Mom was hospitalized, within four or five days Dad would end up in an adjoining room or another floor of the hospital. He would go downhill in a hurry and I would end up with both of them in Loma Linda's cardiac care unit. This happened not once, but three or four times. He relied on her, I think, much more than most people realized. He really *could not* get along without her there. He would, literally, worry himself sick when anything happened to her.

17

The Sound of Music

ad could play any kind of musical instrument, especially anything with strings. He probably could have even played all the kitchen utensils—he was that talented. I didn't know he could play a fiddle until we were up in Marysville, California, at a square dance following a barn raising. I always knew he could call a mean square dance—he had done that in a couple of his movies—but I was really surprised when he borrowed someone's fiddle and played a super hoedown.

Dad was a great performer with a beautiful voice, but he never really learned to read music; his ability was all natural and he played by ear. You could hum something and he would pick it up instantly. This was also true of Mom. If you hummed something for her, she would ask you what key you wanted it in; then she would sit down at the piano and play it effortlessly. I guess most people tend to think of my mother as an actress first or perhaps an author. But among the many facets of her talent was her amazing songwriting ability. She could turn any experience into a song. Her first copyrighted song was *Just a Tear of Regret*. She wrote it as her first marriage ended, and the copyright year is 1928. She was just sixteen and her name was Francis Fox. She said that her next song was stolen by the people who offered to publish it and no other song appeared under her name for many years. When I asked her about it, she couldn't remember submitting another song for copyright until she became Dale Evans and was writing with her former husband, Dale Butts.

When she first came to Hollywood, Mom wrote a light-hearted song, "Ah, Ha, San Antone," which the Sons of the Pioneers performed in the John Wayne movie, *Rio Grande*. The Pioneers also recorded it, and even though she performed it at rodeos occasionally—especially if she was in Texas—it was their recording that made it a hit.

Children in Sunday schools across the country still sing *The Bible Tells Me So,* with its familiar opening lines, "Have Faith, Hope and Charity, that's the way to live successfully. How do I know? The Bible tells me so." The song was written for an episode of *The Roy Rogers Show*. Mom and Dad were the owners of the series, and there was no music budget, so they couldn't afford musicians. The plot required a song to be sung to a little girl whose Daddy is in jail; she's sad and needs her day brightened. Mom had to come up with something in an impossibly short time—about 20 minutes. As she told the story, she retired to her dressing room and asked God to give her a song. Twenty minutes later she left her dressing room, sat down at the piano, and filmed the scene, singing her new song. To me, that kind of talent can only be characterized by that well-worn phrase, "God-given." Certainly Mom always felt that was precisely where the song came from.

Happy Trails also came to her very quickly. Mom wrote the song in 1950 just after Robin's birth. It was inspired in part by Mom's mother. She had recently visited the Grand Canyon and had told Mom all about it. Mom started thinking about the guides who take the mules down those steep canyon trails and the call that they would use, which was sort of like a yodel. And that, in turn, led her to start thinking about Ferde Grofé's *Grand Canyon Suite*. Borrowing a rhythm from that classical masterpiece, Mom went to work, and half an hour later *Happy Trails* was born. The title was easy, because Dad often signed autographs, "Happy Trails, Roy Rogers."

Mom wrote the song for a very practical reason. At that time, Dad was using a standard, *Don't Forget Smiles Are Made Out of the Sunshine,* as his theme song. But because a lot of other people had recorded that song, it never felt personal enough to either of them. Mom always said Dad deserved his own song, so she wrote it.

Happy Trails became more than just their theme song. It came to personify their very philosophy of life:

> Who cares about the clouds when we're together?
> Just sing a song and bring the sunny weather.

That about sums up the way she looked at the world. Just before she died, it was voted the all-time No. 1 TV theme song. That was wonderful because she lived long enough to know it. I am only sorry Mom couldn't have seen the close of the Salt Lake City Winter Olympics where her song was used so very appropriately. It was absolutely thrilling to hear thousands of voices singing *Happy Trails* as the Olympics came to a close, and I know Mom would have been thrilled beyond description.

18

My Career in Show Business

At one time I really wanted to be in show business—I was such a ham! Music came so easy for Mom and Dad; all it took was for someone to hum a tune and they would play it on the piano or guitar, in any key. Just picking out a melody was difficult for me and transposing the simplest tune could be an all-day project. I was not a natural singer; but I loved music and I worked hard to improve my singing and playing. Mom told my husband, Larry, that she never saw a kid who couldn't carry a tune at all work so hard, to the point that I became a more than credible singer. I finally got good enough that Mom and Dad would let me sing with them. By age sixteen I was singing with the Frontiersmen. Then I was offered that opportunity to appear on the *Ed Sullivan Show*—truth or dare time.

I have always been able to say that I passed the chance because my fiancé didn't want me to take it. In fact, he forbade me to go to New York and said that if I did, the engagement was over. But saying that I let Bill dictate my future career is too easy an out. A better and probably more accurate explanation is that I had grown up in a home with two musical geniuses. When you grow up around people who have natural talent and you know *you* don't have it . . . well, it was an easy decision for me to make.

But that isn't to say that I haven't done plenty of singing and dancing in my life.

We never went around the block that Dad wouldn't burst into song and would usually have us join in. By the time I was a pre-teen, we kids often went on tour with Mom and Dad—and they worked us into the act.

I was thirteen the year we went to Hawaii; this was before it was a state. What an incredible experience that was. There was just Linda Lou and me, and Dodie, who was just a toddler at the time—just us girls. Our first stop was at the Hana Guest Ranch on the island of Maui. Mom immediately enrolled us all in hula classes and decided to incorporate us doing the hula into the act when we got to Honolulu. Dodie hadn't been with us a year yet but Mom had written a song for her called *Chicki Wicki Choctaw*. The music would start to play and Dodie would toddle onto the stage in her little grass skirt—the audience loved it and Dodie.

But my greatest memory of that trip isn't the hula lessons or the performances—it was that Linda Lou and I discovered room service. We arrived in Honolulu and were whisked away to the Royal Hawaiian Hotel. As usual, Mom and Dad took off to visit the local children's hospital and then start rehearsals. Virginia Peck was taking care of Dodie, so Linda Lou and I were sort of on our own. We were still under Dad's lifelong rules—don't get dirty and don't get in trouble. Well, what trouble could we possibly get into? There was the ocean, a hotel full of interesting people, and an elevator that we got to run. We'd never seen one of those before because everywhere else we had stayed there was an operator who ran the elevator. We thought this really was paradise. For the first time ever, we were sort of on our own. And sometime that day, we figured out how to call room service. We must have ordered four fresh pineapples that day and then we ordered prime rib—we'd just pick up the phone, place an order and food was brought—this was great! When Dad got back that night and discovered the unbelievable bill that his daughters had run up, we thought he was going to explode. We *definitely* got in trouble for that little caper—but, oh, we had eaten well that day!

I joined Mom and Dad in Toronto the summer of 1954 at the Canadian Exhibition. I was only there for the first week of their three-week stand, but I fell in love with the Canadian people. It was a great show, with lots of international circus acts, and on our day off we went to Niagara Falls. There wasn't anyone along to chaperon me and I probably had a lot more freedom than a fourteen-year-old should, but the circus performers kept an eye on me. Most of them had literally been born in a trunk and they traveled as family units. I was fascinated by how they communicated, this mini-United Nations—there were acts from France, Egypt, Spain, England, and us. It was great.

We had a ball the summer of 1956, when all seven of us went on tour with Mom and Dad. Being the oldest, I was the keeper of the lists. Mom wrote out a list for each of us, detailing everything we had with us—how many pairs of socks and underwear, how many curlers, you get the idea. It was my job, as we were packing to go from one hotel to another, to make sure that we left with the same number of items that we arrived with. When you've got seven kids of all ages, the logistics were incredible.

That summer we played state fairs in Cincinnati, Ohio and Des Moines, Iowa. While we were on our way to our first stop, the boys' pregnant mouse gave birth in mid-air. The stewardesses were hysterical and Dad was furious. But that kind of thing was par for the course when you traveled with our family. Mom had worked her usual magic and we were being paid to be part of the act—everyone had something to do. The two little girls had a separate number of their own. Mom adapted *Chicki Wicki Chocktaw* so that the two girls would come out on stage in Indian outfits—even though Debbie was Korean and Puerto Rican. They were adorable and, as expected, the audience loved them. We three older girls sang a number that Mom had arranged, *The Cowgirl Polka*. Mom had arranged and choreographed the number. By "choreographed" I mean we moved, sort of like the girl groups in the '60s, a little step here and there, some hand motions—not much. The boys would do a comedy bit with Dad and then we would all join in to sing the finale, *Happy Trails*. Mom was the real creative force behind the shows. She designed the costumes, arranged the music, put together the medleys they sang, and did the choreography.

Performance days were insanity. The alarms would go off in our various hotel rooms. I was usually the one assigned to make sure that no one overslept, so I knocked on the boys' door and checked with whoever was helping the little girls—sometimes Mary Jo Rush, Art's wife, sometimes Pat Brady's wife, Fayetta, sometimes Larry Kent's wife, Dorothy, and sometimes one of our housekeepers. We usually met downstairs for breakfast, then Mom and Dad would leave for rehearsals or to do promos at the local radio or TV stations. These were the days before blow dryers were portable, so we would usually have our hair put up in rollers and do homework or whatever else Mom had assigned as our task for the morning. At noon we would head out for the fairgrounds. If there was enough time, we would get to play a couple of games along the midway or we would watch the square dancers at the pavilion. Then we were ushered backstage to await our music cues.

Backstage was total chaos. There were the Sons of the Pioneers, Mom and Dad, the seven of us, and whoever was helping keep us all together. It was wonderful and I loved it. Our cues would sound and we would go out, perform our acts and join the parents for the finale! Then, off to the hotel, dinner, retouches to the hair and costumes, then back to the fairground to do it again for the night performance. By the time *Happy Trails* was performed for the second time that day, we were all ready to go back to the hotel and fall into bed. Ah, the glamour of it all!

That marked the end of my life as a touring performer. By the summer of 1957 I was working at a dress shop in Canoga Park and then later got a job at California Bank. But even though I didn't choose show business as my life's work, I'll always have wonderful memories of my time on stage, both with and without the Rogers Family.

19

Love and Marriage

$\mathcal{H}$aving a bunch of younger sisters and brothers was a trial when you were dating. It was a house rule that you couldn't go out with a boy—not even on a double date or to a sports night—unless Mom and Dad met them first. Almost every time a boy would come by for the first time he would be subjected to my little brothers running through the house screaming, "Cheryl's got a boyfriend, Cheryl's got a boyfriend!"

Once, I asked a boy along to one of Dad's boat races. The races were a couple of hours' drive from where we lived, so it was an all-day outing. I had a crush on this guy, but this was the first time we had been anywhere together.

Dad took Dusty and Sandy in his car while Mom took the rest of us in the station wagon. My date and I were seated all the way in the back on one of those backward-looking seats. The day was spent watching Dad race, eating a picnic lunch, and trying to keep track of younger siblings—*very* romantic. As we were driving home, Dodie, who was about five at the time, looked at my date and said, "You don't want to marry Cheryl, do you?" Ah, the end of the perfect date.

I didn't date many guys that I went to high school with. Most of the guys I dated had graduated several years before I dated them. I liked dating older men because they took me to nice restaurants and treated me like a lady. Boys my own age generally acted like teenage boys and I felt I was above that kind of thing. I had been raised mainly with adults and considered myself their peer. As soon as school was over for the day I was out the door on my way to work.

I didn't attend my senior All Night Party—I didn't see any reason to. I had gone to my friend Jo Ann's party in Long Beach two years before. By the time I graduated, I was engaged and my wedding day was only two weeks away.

A friend of mine, Skip Young, was a good friend of Ricky Nelson's. Skip often appeared on *The Adventures of Ozzie and Harriet* as Ricky's pal Wally. Skip was up at the ranch one day along with a whole group of kids, and he asked me if I knew a nice girl that would like to go out with Ricky. The catch was, I couldn't tell her who she would be going out with. Ricky was a real nice guy, but seemed very shy. I asked my girlfriend Carol if she would join me and a couple of guys for the evening on a blind date—you can't imagine how hard it was to get moms to agree to let their daughters go out when you couldn't tell them who their daughter's escort would be.

Carol agreed to the date and the guys came by Saturday, late afternoon. We went swimming, then we went to Bob's Big Boy Drive-in for dinner. Ricky scrunched down in the back seat, being as inconspicuous as possible. Then we went back home and the guys shot some pool. My girlfriend was thrilled to go out with Ricky but the whole event wasn't romantic or even particularly memorable. To me, it was just another double date.

Robert Blake and I dated several times but we were never really "a couple." I had known him for years, ever since he worked on the Republic lot back when I was a little kid. One time we went to Knott's Berry Farm where we panned for gold and went on the log ride. We had a wonderful time; it was one of the most fun days I can remember. My girlfriend Judy and I made spaghetti one night for Bob and his roommate Dean Stockwell; they were sharing a house in North Hollywood. Again, it was just a casual evening with friends.

Once, Bob asked me to find a date for his good friend, James Darren. They were working on a movie about teen gangs, a very big subject in the mid-'50s. I asked my girlfriend JoAnn if she wanted to spend the weekend with me and told her to bring clothes to spend a day at one of the studios. I drove us to the studio, where Bob had left a pass for us. We spent the day on the lot, watching the filming. We went to lunch together as a group and had a great time.

About three weeks later Bob and I double-dated with James Darren . . . and his wife! They were high school sweethearts, which I thought terribly romantic, but no one could know that she was his wife because the studio demanded that he keep it a secret. Bob told me on the way to the restaurant that they were married. It was a nice dinner and I had a lovely time, but I was upset with Bobby for not telling me about Jimmy being married before I asked JoAnn to go out with him. I didn't want her to be hurt when the news finally broke. Jimmy was a very nice guy. It had to be incredibly hard being married but not allowed to be a couple when out in public. I know the pressure the studio put on Mom and Dad when they went against the studio and got married.

I also dated World Champion rodeo rider Casey Tibbs. I was performing at the Houston Fat Stock Show with Mom and Dad in 1956 where Casey was competing and defending his title as World All-Round Champion. He was very handsome, very nice, and several years older than me. He really swept me off my feet and I was sure that I had found true love. We spent every day together for the week, but when I returned to California, even though he had promised to call, I didn't hear from him. I really had my feelings hurt and confided in my girlfriend Margaret, Glenn Randall's daughter. I knew that Glenn and Casey were friends and that Casey stayed at their house sometimes when he was in California. Margaret found out that Dad had told Casey that he did not want him to call me, ever. I was disappointed in Casey, but furious with Dad.

It was a few months later that I met Bill Rose.

I met Bill at a party on the third of July. I remember there was a huge fire in Chatsworth and it was coming right toward our house. My girlfriend Carol and I were going to a party at another friend's house over in San Fernando. Mom said, "Well sweetheart, if the house isn't here when you get back, spend the night at your grandmother's and we will pick you up tomorrow." So with that cheery advice, off Carol and I went.

When I was singing with the Frontiersmen I didn't want to use the Rogers name. I thought it would seem like I was cashing in. So I chose the stage name Cheryl Rose. Roses are my birth flower, I could keep my initials, and it just sounded like a good "marquee" name. James, our Filipino houseman, was big into numerology and he said that Rose would be very lucky for me. I had been using that name for about a year and a half when I met Bill. As soon as I heard his last name, I knew it was fate. Of course, at seventeen everything is highly dramatic and romantic, and this seemed like Kismet.

Bill was established in his chosen profession and was pointed in the right direction to really make progress in that field. He was a surveyor and dreamed of becoming a civil engineer, which he later did. When we were courting, Bill and I managed to spend at least fifteen minutes together almost every day for seven months. Even though he lived in San Fernando, he worked just ten minutes from my high school. We would meet every day for lunch, then I would go to my job at the bank. This was really heady stuff for a young girl. Every time that Mom would say something about taking things slower, getting more training for a better job—I was working in a bank by that time and singing on weekends—I would remind her that she was married at fourteen when she had no training for any job and that I was an "old maid" compared with her. Poor Mom, I must have been a trial. No, I *know* I was a trial because she told me I was—then and throughout the rest of our lives.

I am often asked why my sisters and I all chose to marry during or immediately following our senior year of high school. I don't mean to speak for my sisters, but I personally don't think that it occurred to us that we shouldn't. Most of our girlfriends did the same.

The night before I was to marry Bill Rose, Mom came to my room and offered to get me an apartment for six months and she would ask her friend Ralph Carmichael to give me a job in his choral group. Or that she would pay my tuition to college if I would give that a try. Maybe she had put off this talk until the last minute because she hoped that I wouldn't actually go through with the wedding. But I reminded her that we had 500 guests coming the next day, that Bill and I had our own apartment, and it was a little late to be having this conversation. I think what precipitated this is that I had been engaged at the ripe old age of fifteen to another boy. Mom, to her credit, went along with it no doubt thinking that it would run its course and die a natural death. She was right and must have thought that history was going to repeat itself. When she realized I was serious, she came through with all manner of inducements . . . all to no avail. I know she wanted me to get married eventually, but she thought I was too young. I think Dad, on the other hand, was just pleased that I had graduated from high school; neither he nor his sisters had made it that far. *That* was the extent of his ambitions for us.

I was one of two valedictorians of my class and had almost always been on the honor roll. I really don't know why they didn't encourage us to get a higher education, but it was not a part of our family culture, not even for Dusty. Dad wanted him to graduate from high school—which he did—and find a good steady trade to go into. I remember a couple of my teachers being upset with me, but it didn't seem to bother anybody else. Now I look back and think what an idiot I was for not getting more education before marrying Bill.

It was a beautiful wedding. I had the wedding that Mom had never had—because she had eloped four times. I was the oldest daughter and the first to marry. We had announced our engagement in October, I graduated in January, and we married on Valentine's Day.

A week or so before the wedding, when I picked up my high school yearbook, the girl standing next to me in line mentioned that she had just come from visiting a mutual friend who had the measles. I didn't pay much attention because I was so excited and busy.

Mom's dressmaker made the most beautiful, and practical, wedding dress for me. I designed it and it fit Mom's criteria, beautiful but versatile. It was an antique satin strapless gown with two floating trains in the back and an Irish lace jacket. The trains could be removed later, the skirt could be shortened, and the jacket could be worn with other dresses—very practical. My bridesmaids were in beautiful rose-red taffeta dresses that a friend had made as her wedding gift. Linda Lou was in the same red taffeta but the top of her dress was trimmed in the same lace as that used in my jacket. Dodie and Debbie were adorable flower girls and one of my godsons was the ring bearer. This was a real Mom-and-Cheryl production.

Bill had been sick with the Asian flu for the week prior to the wedding. He was always slender, but he lost ten pounds with that flu and looked gaunt and drawn—we'd almost had to postpone the wedding. Then, as I was standing at the altar, I got very faint and started to pass out. Mom said it was just nerves and told me to take a few deep breaths and relax.

We had a big reception—the Sons of the Pioneers provided music, while the guests ate wedding cake and drank punch. The next morning, Bill and I started our drive to Big Bear, where we had rented a honeymoon cabin. During the drive, I had one of the worst headaches I have ever had—my eyes hurt so badly that I thought I was going blind. We had finally got checked into our cottage, unpacked our suitcases, and I immediately got violently ill. Again, it must be nerves.

When we woke up the next morning, I was covered all over with little red spots—German measles! We spent most of our honeymoon playing pinochle with friends who lived there in Big Bear.

When I stood next to my friend who had been exposed to the measles, I didn't think anything about it because I had already had the measles. Then, years later, I caught them again with my kids. I am one of the really weird people who can catch the measles repeatedly. Bill and I were very "modern" and we believed in making plans. I had been to my doctor because we weren't going to have babies for at least two or three years. So we did everything we should to prevent getting pregnant, but I got pregnant almost immediately. It was only about three months later that I had my first miscarriage; the doctor said that I must have had the measles when I got pregnant because the baby had never really formed. In some ways I'm thankful for that miscarriage; Mom got the measles when she was in her third month with Robin and she always wondered if that was one of the contributors to Robin's many health problems.

After our dreary honeymoon, Bill and I came back to our apartment in Granada Hills to find his grandparents living there. They had come out from Iowa for the wedding and stayed. We had a one-bedroom apartment and they were with us, off and on, for several weeks!

Bill's four years older than I am. He had been out of school and found a profession that he intended to follow the rest of his life. I hadn't wanted to marry anybody in show business because it's such an unstable business. Either you can't find work at all or you're on location for months at horrid places where you can't take your family. I wanted to marry somebody in a job that was stable, someone who would go to work in the morning and come home at night. So, guess what? Literally only a couple of months after we got married, Bill took a job surveying sites for the Feather River Dam project that would bring water to Southern California. That first year I hardly ever saw him—he was away all the time. I drove up to Reno so that we could celebrate my eighteenth birthday together. Then when he was working at Lake Almanor, I took a Greyhound bus all the way to Northern California to be with him for a few days. Even then, I only saw him at night when he came home from work. We were together and then apart, together and apart as far as his job went.

Because of Bill's job we had a couple of other separations when we only saw each other on weekends. But mainly, we just sort of grew apart as couples often do. He was busy working and I was busy raising kids. Outside of our children, we really didn't have anything else in common and our children were becoming adults. We had been children ourselves when we married, and we just grew apart. Our marriage never got horrible as those of some of our friends did. I didn't want any part of his business; we had four kids. After twenty-one years it was time to change my life.

Once Bill and I split up, Mom told me that I should have known all along that the marriage was doomed. She told me we were too young—after all, look at what happened on our honeymoon. I never quite figured what she meant by that comment. Mom was a great one for hindsight!

But even though my marriage wasn't such a great success, we had four thoroughly delightful children.

Now, I always try to do things in an orderly fashion, so I had my children in a particular order—girl, boy, girl, boy. Lisa is my oldest, born in 1960 when I was nineteen and a half. By the time she was born we were beginning to think we would never be successful at having a child and had actually started talking about adopting. Lisa was quite tiny but as healthy as could be. She was a miracle to her father and me. She came at twelve minutes after midnight on the second of January. Bill called everybody that we knew and maybe some we didn't. The only thing that most of them found out was that it was a girl. Lisa was the first girl in his family in three generations, so the birth was especially thrilling for him. He called people and just babbled that it was a girl, a girl, a girl.

During most of my pregnancy with Brian we were living in Hawaii, but I came back to the mainland before he was born. I had received word that my Granddaddy Wilkins was dying and I wanted to see him. In those days, doctors told women not to fly if you were past your sixth month of pregnancy, so I waited until the last weekend that they would allow me to fly and I came back to be with my family; Bill remained in Hawaii. At that time, Bill was the assistant project manager for Henry Kaiser's Hawaii Kai Project—they were building houses in the swamp.

Lisa had been really sick while we were over there and they thought she had spinal meningitis. Luckily, she didn't, but we were only reassured after a spinal tap and many other tests. At the same time, I was undergoing a difficult pregnancy. In fact, I thought that I had miscarried again, but here came Brian, hale and hearty.

When I was barely three months pregnant with Kim, my appendix ruptured. It was not until six weeks later that I got out of the hospital. I was four-and-a-half months pregnant and weighed 101 pounds. I looked like I had been in a concentration camp. I learned later that my condition had been touch-and-go for months but I was so sick I really didn't care. Poor Mom—she really hung in there on that one. I know she was praying double-time. But despite all the suffering, Kimmy was born perfectly healthy. The doctors, however, warned me that if I had another baby I was going to die. I replied that that was perfectly fine with me—I was ready to stop at three!

I asked them to tie my tubes so I couldn't have another baby. They told me that they couldn't do that, I was much too young. I was twenty-two with three babies and begged them to do *something*. You'd think they would have done something; after all, they had told me I was going to die if I had another baby. I also told them that we had tried all of the things that you are supposed to do to keep from having babies and none of those techniques had worked. In fact, a couple of the prescriptions made me feel so bad that being pregnant was easier.

And they didn't work the fourth time either, because twenty months later, my youngest son Mark came along. You'll be relieved to know that I didn't die—but it was a really difficult pregnancy! I was in bed for the last three months of the pregnancy with three little ones under the age of four in the house. I could never afford to hire someone to help. It was my sister Mimi who helped me immeasurably—boy, I don't know what I would have done without her. I also had a couple of my close girlfriends who helped me.

Bill and I were living in Sylmar at the time. We were finally able to buy a house after Brian was born. Bill had quit his job about two months after Lisa and I returned to California and he relocated to be with us prior to Brian's birth. Brian was born at Kaiser Hollywood. Because we lived in Canoga Park, quite a distance away, he was almost born on the freeway. When we had Kimmy, we had just bought the house in Sylmar and she was born at Holy Cross. Mark was born at Valley Presbyterian—every kid was born at a different hospital!

Lisa is very much like I am—always pushing the limits. This thoroughly delighted Mom and Dad who got to say many an "I told you so." As Dad always said whenever I complained about her wild behavior, "You deserve her." She was really bright and caught on to everything at school so quickly. Her poor teachers felt she was a real trial. We let her skip a half a year and they wanted to put her up even more. They told us she was bored. I knew the feeling—I'd been exactly the same way when I was a kid. At the same time I remembered Mom's experience and I didn't want Lisa being the youngest by too many months. I knew how hard it was when you were in with kids who were a lot older, and she was always small for her age.

I think it worked out well. Lisa is a divorced, single parent dating a very nice man. She is an interior designer by avocation and is very gifted in that field but has never pursued it as a career. She has worked in banking and a couple of other fields and she currently is managing the office for the Builder's Association in Lake Havasu— so the interior design education is finally of use. Our granddaughter Markayla, bless her heart, is just like her mother and her Nana (me). She is bright, opinionated, and extremely independent.

Brian went into the Army from high school. He can build or take apart anything. He is a motorcycle mechanic, a welder, a house painter. He's a very artistic builder who designs beautiful homes. Brian is divorced and his former wife, Colleen, is raising their three boys—Brian Jr., Mike, and Rob M at Lake Havasu; they're wonderful, active boys who are turning into wonderful young men.

Kimmy married young, and has been married forever. She and Bob got married before Larry and I did, which is more than twenty-two years ago. Bob became diabetic while a teenager; this has caused many health problems over the years. He had a good job in the aerospace industry and Kim was able to be a housewife. Then Bob's health deteriorated to the point he needed a kidney/pancreas transplant. During his illness, Kim provided the health care he needed until he finally got his transplant. Now Bob's doing fine and Kim is a manager at an AM/PM. They adopted Jeremy when he was eighteen months old. Because of the abusive treatment he received prior to his adoption, it was almost two years before he slept through his first night without nightmares. Jeremy just graduated from high school and he recently enlisted in the Army Reserve. We're very proud of him.

Although my last pregnancy was in some ways the most difficult, Mark, from his first day, was a delight. He was a happy, sunny little boy who wanted everyone around him to be happy. He grew up with a fascination with speed. He loved cars, motorcycles, anything that could go really fast—just like my Dad. He turned that passion into a vocation. Mark became editor and publisher of *Off Road* magazine. That's where he met his wife-to-be Shawna. She was in the publishing business, too, working for the same company but a different magazine. They were the perfect couple and were supremely happy in the short time they had together before Mark's sudden death in a racing car accident.

Mark's boys are now ten and eight. Sterling is a fine artist, who loves baseball and soccer. Ashton loves music and soccer. Shawna was married for a short time to a friend of Mark's. They had a son, Maverick, and a daughter, Ramie, before their marriage ended in divorce. Shawna is now a vice-president at her company and I pray that Mark knows how well they're doing. The boys are growing into fine, strong young men thanks to their mother—she is as beautiful inside as she is gorgeous on the outside.

Today, I'm married to my best friend—and one of my oldest friends. Larry Barnett and I have known each other since high school. We even dated a time or two. We went to the local drive-in, along with the rest of Canoga Park High School, we went to a couple of sports nights, and I once took him to a party at actor Steve Cochran's house. He still talks about that one! But things never went any further than that.

Larry will never forget the day he met Mom. I had missed my bus home from school and wandered out to the athletic field hoping to snag a ride home. Football practice was just ending and I saw Larry heading my way. He seemed like a good prospect and I asked him if he could give me a ride home. Since he was already taking one of our friends to his home, Larry said it wouldn't be an inconvenience at all. The three of us got in Larry's car and headed to my house in Chatsworth. When we arrived, I asked if they would like to come in and meet Mom. How could they resist that invitation?

We went up the steps and through the front door where, as Larry still claims, Mom was waiting in ambush for him. Mom allowed me to finish the introductions before asking where the other girl was. And then she proceeded to take Larry apart, brick by brick. You see, one of the cardinal rules of the house was that her daughters did not ride in a car unless there was an equal number of girls and boys. Larry still insists I set him up. Anyway, Mom finished her lecture and then said, "There, I've said my piece. Now can I get you boys something to drink?" You should have seen how quickly he declined the invitation and hit the door, heading for home.

As I've mentioned earlier, I was engaged before I met my first husband, and the other guys that I dated while I was in high school were all older—most of them were *considerably* older. In fact, Bill, who was four years older than I was, was one of the youngest guys I dated while I was in high school. Boys my own age were usually too grabby. I liked going out with older men because they treated me like a lady, and that to me was very important.

While I didn't seem to have a problem getting dates, I didn't have a lot of friends. From the first day that I met him, Larry was the type of friend you could tell anything to and it would never go anywhere. He was just a great guy. When I married Bill, Larry was invited to my wedding. He later told me that he left early, much as he wanted to go to the reception and hear the Sons of the Pioneers. He thought I was nuts for getting married so young. What can I say? Larry's often right about things.

Then Bill and I moved to Hawaii and when we moved back, Larry had left for Hawaii himself, to attend college there. I remember going by and seeing his folks a couple of times because they had adopted a little girl that they named after my sister Debbie. So I did go by and have lemonade or something with his mom after I came back from Hawaii, but he had already left by then.

Then his parents moved and I lost touch with them; I didn't see Larry again until he was divorced and Bill and I were on the brink of divorce. I saw Larry at a reunion committee meeting. Because of working on the reunions our paths crossed a couple more times over the next couple of years.

After I filed for divorce, I took a job working in the office of Congressman Barry Goldwater Jr. There were many events that I was required to attend as his representative. I didn't like to attend them alone but I didn't want to ask a date either—too many complications. So I would call my best friend, Larry, and, if he wasn't traveling on business, he would drive up from the beach and go with me. Then his daughter Kimber needed a place to live. By that time I had left the congressman's office and I was working for a bank in Beverly Hills and living in Mar Vista. Larry traveled a lot; he was a sales manager for a big company. I told him that Kimber could come live with me and finish her senior year at Santa Monica High School. It turned out to have been one of the best decisions I ever made. We saw even more of each other because Kimber was living with me.

I have a Kimberly, and Larry has Kimber Lee—which makes for a little confusion. Kimber has always been Kimber, however. Lee is Larry's middle name, so they gave her his middle name. Her Hawaiian name is Maheolani. His older two girls were born in Hawaii. Kimber is, as Larry says, our Mad Scientist. She is a senior research chemist for Pfizer Pharmaceuticals in Connecticut. Kimber is a delightful young woman and mother. Larry says she talked in her own language when she was little, and I think she still does in a way. When she was working on her doctorate she sent us one of the papers she had written. We never saw her thesis, but the paper we did see might as well have been written in Greek, we would probably have comprehended just as much. So we got used to her telling us, whenever we asked her a question about what she was working on, that we just wouldn't understand. And it's true. She married a great guy, a fellow student and her best friend from the University of Missouri-Rolla. Dale is a wonderful son-in-law. How can you *not* like somebody named Dale?

He is an electrical engineer now working for Electric Boats in New Haven, Connecticut. They have one little girl, Emily, who is delightful, very precocious child. She goes to school on the campus at Pfizer. She is already having a very interesting life and she just turned three.

Kerry, Larry's middle daughter, is just younger than my Mark. She's a fine athlete like her father. She is an independent duty corpsman and has been stationed in Oakland and in San Diego. She volunteered for duty in Antarctica and New Zealand, where she ran the clinic. She was recently promoted to chief and we are very proud of her.

Kathy, the youngest, graduated from high school and then got a certificate as a sound engineer. She was a divorced single parent when she married Frank Macias, an L.A. firefighter who used to work those huge high-rise fires. When the third child was on the way, he took the exam and became an engineer and is studying for the captain's test now that they have four little ones. Our granddaughter Marlene is a really good gymnast—an athlete like her grandpa Larry. Jack and Luke are in the middle and are typical boys. They love sports, especially gymnastics. Elena Michelle was born while I was completing this book. She is grandchild number fourteen! That's a lot of grandchildren, but they are each so different and so wonderful—much nicer than their parents in most cases! But that's probably what all grandparents think.

Larry and I were both occasionally dating other people at the time when Kimber came to live with me. But it finally dawned on us that something serious was happening. I thought, "This is just so comfortable and obviously the right thing to do." So twenty-five years after we met, we were married, on the 27th of December in 1981. It seems as if we have been together always.

The last few years have been difficult on us all. I know I am certainly thankful that he's been here beside me, sometimes propping me up. He was able to develop a friendship with Mom and Dad and was the one who drove them to the emergency room on many a late-night run. Without him I certainly wouldn't be able to do the things I'm doing now. He is supportive. He's a great guy. He's still my best friend.

20

Mom's Steadfast Faith

Toward the end of her life, my Mom might have been better known for her Christian witness than she was for her movies. Through her regular television appearances, she was practically evangelistic, preaching the word of salvation to anyone who would listen. Dad was a Christian also, but I think he looked at religion differently than Mom did. He really was a man of the earth—basic and yet complex. Mom was much more cerebral. When she embraced something it was with all of her being.

Dad told me that he had avoided church for many years when he was younger. When he was a kid they didn't have a local church, just the occasional itinerant preacher who would come in, preach a little, take up a collection, and pass on through. He said he thought they were about on the same level as snake-oil salesmen—in fact, that's what he called them. He said it seemed to be their mission to scare their congregations into repenting. But for Dad, the most offensive thing about these preachers was that they seemed to be in it only for the money, even though the people who came to hear them usually had little. Dad said that he had seen neighbors who couldn't even afford shoes for their kids, yet they were so scared of going to hell that they would give what little they had to these "Elmer Gantry"-type preachers. Trying to get a little money from poor people struck Dad as a very cynical and dishonest thing to do. It soured him on religion for a long time.

Mom was away from the church for many years—when she rebelled, she really rebelled. But then when she married Dad and suddenly became Mom to three little kids, she was determined that this was going to be a marriage and a family that stayed together. As I said earlier, she originally went back to her Baptist roots. Then as we moved from one town to another, Mom changed her church affiliation depending more upon the preacher and his message than upon the denomination of the church. In fact, every time we moved we changed our church affiliation.

Mom was never preachy with people. If you asked her a question, she would tell you what she thought and maybe even suggest what she thought you should do—she wasn't above doing that! But she wasn't somebody who would plunk down next to you and say, "Oh, by the way, I'm a Christian. Do you know Jesus?" That was definitely not how Mom did things. Her newfound Christianity made a difference in her—in her attitude—at home and everywhere she went. She glowed with the Spirit. I think this change in her made Dad curious; he wanted to know what was going on with her.

Dad didn't go to church with us in the beginning. But in only a few weeks, he became so enthralled with Mom's new attitude that he began coming along. Eventually, he and I were baptized on the very same Sunday morning.

It's interesting that we were going to a Baptist church, because Mom and Dad had sent me to a Catholic school. It was more than a little confusing for me because the Catholics thought that only they were saved and the Baptists thought that only *they* were saved. But Mom didn't believe in divisions in Christianity; she always looked at things from a uniquely personal perspective. Mom felt that the only thing it took was what it said in the Bible—if you believed in God and that Jesus was his son—and you proclaimed that belief, well, that was all it took. All of this friction between the churches she felt was absolute nonsense.

When we would spend weekends on Catalina Island, we always went to the Catholic church because that was the only one there at the time. Not only would Mom happily attend Mass, she would take communion. She figured she had been baptized, so she was entitled—even though she wasn't Catholic! I was always so embarrassed, but it didn't give her a second thought.

Catholic? Baptist? They worshipped the same God and recognized Jesus as His son, so why was there a difference? I would say, pleadingly, "But you didn't go to confession, did you?" And she would reply, "Of course not! I'm a Baptist—I don't *have* to go to confession!"

Mom reduced religion to its simplest truths; you were either saved or you weren't. If you were saved you should be able to go into any Christian church that you wanted to and take communion at the altar. That's how she lived her life.

Larry was raised a Catholic. His grandmother was a Flynn from County Cork. He was an altar boy when he was little and his grandmother thought that he would make a splendid priest. He says that he used to conduct pretend masses when he was a little guy.

Larry and I took Mom and her companion Martha Brown to a big church in Thousand Oaks for the funeral of Dad's former stunt-double, Joe Yrigoyen, who was a Basque and a Catholic. Mom was sitting there in her wheelchair and fully participating in the service. Mom adored the Catholic Mass. She often said that she loved the form and grandeur of the ritual. As the priest prepared for communion, Mom said, "Martha, take me down there." Larry couldn't believe it. "What are you doing?" he said. I just sat quietly; I knew what was coming.

Mom had Martha her wheel her down to the rail to take communion. Larry had never seen a non-Catholic take communion at a Catholic Church—most people haven't.

Larry and Mom would have incredible "debates" arguing the merits of Catholic vs. Baptist. They also discussed the changes in the now "modern" Catholic Church: women participating in the Mass, the move away from the use of Latin.

Larry turned to me and said, "Well, I guess that just shows how much the Church has changed." I said, "Oh no, she has always done this" and told him about our experience in Catalina. He was so funny—I really think he expected for the roof to open and God to send down a bolt of lightning. After taking communion, Mom came back and sat next to Larry for the rest of the Mass. When Mass was over and we returned to the car, Larry told her that she wasn't supposed to take communion unless she went to confession first. She gave her usual response, with just a slight change. "I don't have to go to confession, I'm Presbyterian."

Dad wasn't like that. He had kept the church at arm's length, not only because of his lifelong distrust of the evangelists of his boyhood, but also because of all the terrible injustice, pain, and inequity he saw in the world.

He made it a lifelong practice to visit kids in the hospitals of just about every town or city he visited. And he was often devastated by what he saw. He once said to Mom, "How can you expect me to believe in a God that allows children to suffer like that?" Robin's pain and death were a real trial to him. He hadn't been a Christian for very long and he had a horrible time reconciling her reality with his young faith. I think that's when he made peace within himself and decided that he wouldn't understand a lot of things until he was standing in front of God—then he would finally understand.

He could deal with a sick child who was dying from cancer, however, because, in effect, he was "playing Roy Rogers," and that little bit of distance helped him withstand the pain of the awful things he saw. And he was incredible. I often watched these kids gain strength just from his being there.

When Mom was sick and I went to Portland, Oregon, with him, we went to a burn ward at a local hospital. We were shown into the room of a little brother and sister who had gotten caught in a fire. Their wounds were horrible, truly awful, but Dad soon had them smiling and even laughing. When we got out of the hospital and back down in the car, he broke down and sobbed. When he was up there he was someone else, a source of entertainment, strength, and happiness. He gave them the feeling—however fleeting—that they were normal, healthy kids.

I think the irony of the whole thing is that while these experiences caused him to doubt God, his actions were the very personification of Christian charity. I don't know that he ever completely reconciled his ambivalent feelings, but once he joined the church, he began to turn over some of that doubt to God. From then on, he attended church with us every week. The rest of us, on the other hand, went to church several times a week.

Mom was very pragmatic, and she was the leader in all things church-related, far more so than Dad. Dad believed in God but he kept his own counsel. Mom, bless her heart, loved going up to the cemetery that would be their final resting place—it's such a beautiful location and it brought her great comfort. She would sit there and write or think or pray. She was always trying to get Dad to go with her. He always answered, "I'll be there soon enough and long enough, so no thank you!" When she spoke about how it would be in Heaven, she always talked about sitting at the feet of Jesus and listening to the angels' choir. Dad, on the other hand, wanted to know if Trigger and his German shorthair Sam were going to be there. I think these two diverse ideas of what the hereafter is like absolutely define the differences in my parents!

Mom encouraged us to go to any of our friends' churches. At one time or another we have probably belonged to, or at least visited, just about every Christian denomination. Mom and Dad became Presbyterians at the end of their lives because Bill Hansen was the minister at Church of the Valley and Mom really thought the world of him—with good reason. He was the greatest friend and the most wonderful man; among other things, he married Larry and me. He's an exceptional human being, the type of Christian who seems to have an inner glow. The Reverend Billy Graham is like that, too; he possesses an inner light that is just incredible.

Mom and Dad were very good friends with the Rev. Graham and accompanied him on two or three crusades across the United States and in Europe. I think the athlete that Billy had been really attracted Dad. Billy is very much a man's man, and he is so big—physically and spiritually. I couldn't believe his size. The first time he came out to Encino, I was playing tennis with one of my girlfriends. Dad and Mom walked out on the tennis court with this man and all I could think was, "He's so tall!" Of course, he has such charisma that you feel he is bigger than life. He had been a very good college basketball player in his younger days. And he was so nice. Unlike the preachers that Dad had met when he was a kid, Dad and I agreed that Billy Graham is the genuine article.

Once Mom and Dad started going back to church, they helped form the Hollywood Christian Group. Other founders and members included Tim Spencer, one of the founders of the Sons of the Pioneers and one of Dad's oldest friends; Jimmy Dodd, the host of the *Mickey Mouse Club*; and actress Jane Russell. The Hollywood Christian Group was made up of actors, singers, cameramen, grips, hairdressers—anybody in the movie industry was welcome to come. They met once a month, originally at the homes of members and later at the Roosevelt Hotel in Hollywood. It was a good-size group with a lot of ebb and flow. They got a lot of really interesting people to come and speak to them.

We had a lot of those meetings at our house, both when we were at Encino and in Chatsworth. I remember Ethel Waters coming and singing. Mom just loved her. She was a huge stage star and one of the few African American movie stars of her generation. But she spent the last years of her life with the Billy Graham Crusade. Her signature song was *His Eye is on the Sparrow*. Ethel Waters and Mom had been friends since Mom had been a band singer back in Chicago. Mom always talked about her, although I had never gotten to meet her. I was in high school when she came out to attend the group and sang. Mom and Dad were members all the years they lived in the Los Angeles area.

There are still chapters of the Hollywood Christian Group at Paramount Studios, and at CBS studios, on the old Republic lot. It really says something that these groups are still going strong after fifty years. Mom and Dad both had so much of an impact on so many lives.

Our friend Jim Rogers, whom I spoke of earlier, only got to know Mom maybe the last three years of her life. We had dinner with him not too long ago and he said, "You know, I really miss your Mom. I didn't know her that well and I didn't see her that many times but she is somebody you miss." Almost everybody who ever had any contact with her feels the same way; she was so dynamic that she left a hole in our lives. Even at the end, when she definitely was not at the top of her game, she still had more oomph than most people do in their forties. Her faith in God was one of the elements that gave Mom that inner glow. But it also came from the fact that she loved people. She wanted to know everything about you because you were interesting—how could anyone resist that?

The entire Rogers family in Mom and Dad's living room in Apple Valley—1998. There are lots more of us now. I won't even try to name everyone. Larry and I are in the middle of the group. My youngest son, Mark, is the second from the right in the top row. Brian is seated 4th from the left (with Brian Jr. on his lap). Kim is two places to the right of Brian (Jeremy is on her lap). Lisa is the first one on the right in the front row.

I don't know where this 1946 photo was taken but it shows me with a very small Dusty, his godfather Leo Khoury, Mrs. Christensen, Linda Lou and Virginia Peck.

Three hula lessons and Mom has us performing in front of the audience in Honolulu. Me, Mom, Linda Lou and Dad in his Hawaiian cowboy outfit—good thing it was a comedy song. We were joined in Hawaii by The Whippoorwills who provided our musical accompaniment. (1953)

One of the few family photographs with the seven of us. This was taken on the fence at Chatsworth just after Debbie joined our family. Me, Linda Lou, Mimi, Dusty, Sandy, Dodie and Debbie with Mom and Dad. (1956)

Picture of me with most of our kids taken in the courtyard of the museum in 1999. (standing in back row from left) Frank and Kathy (Barnett) Macias, Coleen and Mike Rose, Jack Macias, Kerry Barnett, Marlene Macias, Bob and Kim (Rose) Comer, Kimber (Barnett) and Dale Rundlett. (sitting in front row) Rob and Brian Rose, Brian Rose Jr., me, Lisa and Markayla Rose, and Jeremy Comer. (photographer, J. R.)

A very rare shot with just the six of us as adults with Mom and Dad, Thanksgiving 1983. Dusty, Mimi, Linda Lou, me, Tom and Dodie.

Linda and I join Mom and Dad in celebrating Robin's first birthday. (1951)

The seven of us with Mom and Dad in the living room of the Chatsworth house. Mimi, Dusty, Sandy, Dodie and Debbie, Linda Lou and me. (1957)

Linda, Mom and me in the first and last matching outfits Mom made us. This photo was taken at the ponds in front of our Hollywood house.

Saying grace around the table in the dining room of the
Chatsworth house. Actor/sculptor/furniture maker, George
Montgomery made the table for us in 1953.

Dad and Mom, Linda and me in 1948 on the balcony of the
Hollywood house on Ivarene. This house burned down just as
this book was being completed in 2003.

Dad in front of the
White Oak house.
(1942)

Dad and our
Dalmatian, Duke,
in front of the
house on Longridge
(1945)

Dad signed only one of my
photos "Dad" – normally, he
signed "Roy Rogers & Trigger."

Mom signed this
picture to me
before she and
Dad were married.

This is one of my
favorite photos of
Dad and me. (1942)

Dad with Debbie
and Dodie, still
playing horsey.
(1957)

"Outlaws of Paradise Valley" episode of *The Roy Rogers Show*. Pat Brady teaches my character how to make pancakes while Mom and Dad look on. (1954)

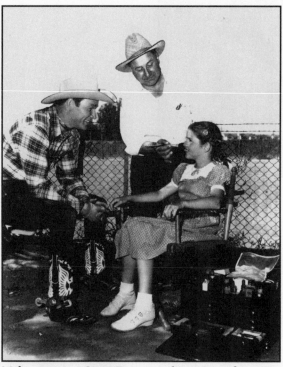

Makeup artist, Steve Drum, makes me up for my screen debut and big scene in *Trail of Robin Hood*. (1950)

I'm standing next to Jack Holt with an autograph book in my hands. This is my big scene—well, my *only* scene. Next to Mr. Holt is the film's costar, Penny Edwards. Kneeling in the front left is costar Carol Nugent. (1950)

Under that hat is a very bald head. Dad and me shortly after I was adopted. (1940)

Dad greets me at the airport in Houston where I joined he and Mom for the Houston Fat Stock Show. (1956)

Dad started me out early advertising Roy Rogers products. (1946)

A rare photo of Dad in a mustache. We are dancing at the party following the premiere of *Jonathan Livingston Seagull*.

Dad was always clowning around and was a big practical joker. Here he hangs me out to dry. (1941)

Dad joins Linda Lou and me at "Kiddie Land" amusement part in Studio City. This was a neat little park that was really close to both Republic Studios and our house on Longridge. (1946)

This was one of the last photo layouts I was in before I got married. Mom is serving sundaes to me and Linda. (1957)

Linda Lou and me in Dale's studio dressing room a couple of years after she became Dad's costar. (1945)

(The studio PR department set up a photo shoot with
Allan "Rocky" Lane taking me out on my 10th birthday.) (1950)

We visit Allan's horse Black Jack (One of my favorite
horses).

We went to a double feature matinee at the Hitching Post Theater in
Hollywood. The first film starred Dad and the second starred Allan.

I'm atop Trigger with Glenn Randall holding the reins. (1945)

Dad and I talk with one of the Ringling Brothers clowns who worked with Dad in *Along the Navajo Trail*. (1945)

Linda Lou and me atop Little Trigger. This is the only time I can recall being on him.

Director John English (Dad's favorite director) lets Linda Lou and me
see what the camera sees on the set at Republic. Of course, Dad had
to hold us up so we could get a good view. (1945)

I get to ride Trigger. (1946)

Dad on Trigger leads my pony, Blondie, for a ride in the Van Nuys wash behind Glenn Randall's ranch. The look on my face says I wanted to do it myself! (1943)

We always had animals around. Dad and I are up at the racing pigeon's coop behind the Longridge house. Note all the pigeons roosting on the roof in the background.

Dad feeding our pet baby squirrel, Smarty Pants.

21

Trigger

*I*n 1946, Mom and Dad co-starred in a movie titled *My Pal Trigger*. To movie audiences, that beautiful golden palomino was just as important a part of the Roy Rogers movies as Roy was. And Trigger was important to Dad, too; they weren't just co-workers, or horse and master, they were, as that movie title correctly suggested, pals.

I'm happy to say that Trigger was *my* pal, too. Although Dad owned him, Trigger lived in the stables of Dad's good friend Glenn Randall, who became known all over Hollywood as one of the best horse trainers of them all.

Glenn's daughter Margaret and I were good friends. I remember the many times she and I would go horseback riding around the Van Nuys wash. The wash was a large sandy area formed when the Los Angeles River occasionally flooded and cut a swath across the San Fernando Valley. In the beginning Margaret rode one of her Dad's horses, and I rode my Shetland pony, Blondie, but as I got older, I sometimes got to ride Trigger—unchaperoned. Can you imagine that happening today?

One of our favorite jaunts was to ride across the wash from their house on Longridge over to a little mom-and-pop store, located on Woodman next to the railroad tracks. When we got there, we'd tie the horses to the hitching post and later I would share whatever treat or snack I bought for myself with Trigger. He particularly loved getting a bite of my mayonnaise sandwich and a sip of my Coca-Cola. He could actually hold the bottle in his mouth and drink it down!

Trigger also liked to drink Dad's coffee, and Dad didn't seem to mind sharing, either. At times Trigger seemed more goat than horse—he would eat almost anything. We probably should have never fed him food like that, but my philosophy at the time was that if I could have a treat, Trigger could have a treat. After all, he was my pal.

Trigger started out life as a movie rental horse. The first time that we know he appeared in a movie was with Olivia De Havilland on his back in the opening scenes of the 1938 classic *The Adventures of Robin Hood*, co-starring Errol Flynn. He was a registered palomino and his name was Golden Cloud. He was one gorgeous horse, as everybody who has ever seen him on the screen or in a photo knows. More than that, he was a great horse with a wonderful disposition. He was about three-fourths thoroughbred and a little bit what Dad said was a "cold-blooded mare"—that's an old horseman's word for a mutt; just a mixture of breeds. Dad always told me that there was a genuine connection between the two of them, right from the first time he sat in the saddle. Dad had a gift for handling most animals, but he said there was some sort of instant communication between him and Trigger. In Dad's case, it was love at first sight.

Now although Dad became a great horseman, he hadn't grown up with horses. Back in Duck Run, there was an old plow horse that he occasionally rode to school on, but they didn't have money to spend on an animal that couldn't earn its own upkeep. Dad had never done any serious riding before he got into the movies, but he was a truly gifted athlete, who caught onto the basic principles very quickly. Even the experts—the rodeo cowboys and stuntmen—always said that of all the movie cowboys, nobody sat a horse like Ken Maynard, Ben Johnson—and Dad.

Trigger had more than a little to do with helping Dad acquire that expertise. Dad worked with some great stuntmen and wranglers. He was what they call a "quick study" and it didn't take him long to pick out the horsemen who he thought rode best and then to figure the mechanics of what they were doing that he liked. He then set himself the task of copying what they were doing. Dad and Trigger would work together for hours on end until they could anticipate the other's demands. Of course, having the most photogenic horse that was ever on the silver screen didn't hurt the popularity of this new duo.

Dad always credited Trigger with saving his career. Dad happened to be in the right place at the right time when he overheard a conversation that Republic was looking for someone to cast in their next Western. Gene Autry's contract was being renegotiated and he and the studio hadn't reached agreement yet. Dad went across the street and, with a little luck, he got through the front gate, auditioned, and got the lead in *Under Western Stars*. Gene and the studio finally agreed on the terms of his new contract and Gene returned to work.

By the time Gene returned to Republic, several months had passed and I think Dad had already made three or four films. Dad loved to tell the story of how the studio head came to him when Dad was trying to negotiate a raise in his contract and in essence told him, "Thanks, but no thanks. You've been good but we don't need you any more. Besides, we can put anybody on Trigger and they'll look great."

Dad replied, "No you can't put anybody on Trigger—he's my horse, I'm buying him!"

And he really was. Almost from the minute Dad laid eyes on Trigger, he knew that horse was something very, very special. So, even though he didn't make much money, he decided to buy the four-year-old stallion from his owners, Hudkins Brothers. Dad and Ace Hudkins had struck up a deal for Dad to make payments while Ace continued to rent Trigger to Republic—but he wouldn't let them put another cowboy on him—until the last payment had been made. It took a couple of years for Dad to make all the payments—after all, he was making $75 a week and he paid $2,500 for that horse! In the early 1940s that was a pretty steep price to pay for any horse and more than one friend of Dad's told him that he'd been taken. But Dad knew they had something special together and he didn't want to run the risk of having some other cowboy riding Trigger in a movie. When I later told Larry what Dad had paid for Trigger, he didn't want to believe me. But while I was working in the backroom of the Museum, I came across a copy of the original bill of sale. I even placed a copy of it in an edition of the museum newsletter.

So even though it took years to pay for him completely, Dad knew that the horse was worth it. Without a doubt, Trigger was the best investment Dad ever made.

Trigger, or the "Old Man" as he was sometimes called, was not a trick horse. His job was to do pretty much what he did with Olivia De Havilland—just stand there and look beautiful. In fact, although he was always billed as "The Smartest Horse in the Movies," he never did do but a couple of stunts. He was great for running scenes, and he could rear better than any horse I ever saw. Dad always told me that he was never afraid of Trigger falling over while rearing. Trigger would stand on his hind legs while reaching towards the sky with his front legs—that horse could stand in an almost perpendicular position and he looked magnificent. When I look at some of those shots in the movies, I'm amazed that Dad could stay on Trigger's back—and look so comfortable doing it.

Old Trigger remained Dad's favorite, but there were actually three Triggers. Dad bought Little Trigger (the "Little Horse") a couple of years after he bought Old Trigger. He purchased the second horse primarily to spare wear and tear on Old Trigger. He wanted a horse that he would take on the road; he only used Old Trigger for the movies. Dad never publicly admitted that there was more than one Trigger. He always said that he didn't want to confuse the little kids who loved Trigger. The fans knew about Trigger Jr.—the studio even had a contest to name him when Dad first got him—but Little Trigger was a "secret."

When Glenn Randall became Dad's horse trainer, more magic occurred. The Little Horse was, according to Dad, Glenn, and other knowledgeable people, just about the smartest horse any of them could remember seeing. After just a few tries, the Little Horse seemed to know exactly what Dad or Glenn wanted him to do. He had more than a hundred cues for tricks he could perform or dances he could do and he didn't seem to forget them.

Dad and Glenn housebroke the Little Horse. Now, Dad had a horse he could take into kids' hospitals, into theaters and occasionally into City Hall. Kids adored him and sometimes Dad would even give them little rides but always with very close supervision.

Old Trigger co-starred in all 82 of the movies Dad made between 1938 and 1952. He also appeared in all 100 TV episodes of *The Roy Rogers Show*. In fact, the only one of Dad's films he wasn't in was *Mackintosh and T.J.*, which was released in 1974. Trigger had died on July 3, 1964.

But the Little Horse was the one that traveled and he did most of the tricks. He didn't appear in many movies, but do you remember that scene in the Bob Hope/Jane Russell movie *Son of Paleface* where Bob Hope is trying to share a bed with Trigger, and Trigger keeps pulling the blanket off Bob with his teeth? That was the Little Horse. There are scenes in an earlier film, *Don't Fence Me In*, where Trigger is dancing; once again, that's the Little Horse.

The Little Horse was considerably smaller than Old Trigger; if you put their photographs side by side, it's very easy to tell the difference between them. He was also a much lighter palomino.

Glenn and Dad came up with ideas and then they would work together with the Little Horse. As a kid, watching it all, it never seemed to me that it took them long at all to teach him a new stunt; he was so smart and caught on so quickly. You really got the sense that not only did he want to please Dad and Glenn, he also was having fun doing it.

But the Little Horse could also be the most ornery horse you can imagine. On several occasions, at rodeos and shows, Dad had to excuse himself to the audience, explain that horses were sometimes like children, and use his quirt, a leather-covered stick he used to give cues, on the Little Horse's ankles. He never beat him or anything like that, but he would give him a couple of good snaps. Dad always explained that it was to get his attention. Of course, for his part, the Little Horse wasn't as considerate and had been known to leave teeth marks along Dad's forearm where he had munched him. He was just too smart and seemed to figure that when he was in front of a crowd, Dad wouldn't do anything—he was just like an ornery little kid.

He would munch us too, if he got the chance. I never went by the Little Horse's stall if I could help it. If I did, I'd carry an apple, so maybe the horse would eat it instead of me. He didn't particularly like kids and he didn't like women. But he loved the spotlight and sometimes tried to have it all to himself.

I love Dad's story about the night performance of Dad and the Little Horse's most classic bit. The way it was supposed to go: they are riding along and a shot rings out. Dad is wounded and he falls off the horse. But loyal Trigger won't leave him. *Another* shot rings out and this time the horse is wounded, too. So Trigger lies down beside Dad, with one leg in the air, and they quietly die. At the climax of the act, there would be a small spotlight beaming directly on them. Otherwise, the stadium was in total darkness. Over the speakers would come the plaintive sound of *Taps*.

Now, the audience might have found this act touching and moving in the extreme, but the Little Horse just thought it was funny—he felt that it was the perfect time to pull a practical joke on Dad. Little Trigger knew *Taps* and that became his cue to start the game—a game called "Leave Roy Alone in the Arena!" When they fell together, side by side, Dad had to hold tight to the reins. He knew if he didn't, Trigger would inch away from him in the darkness and then when the light came on, Dad would be there by himself! Dad said he could *swear* that horse was trying to leave him!

One night, Dad fell and he reached for the reins—and couldn't find them in the dark. *Taps* was playing and he knew when it got to a certain note that the horse was going to be gone. Desperately, Dad lunged in the darkness and, luckily, was able to grab hold of the saddle horn. Well, when the lights came on, there was Trigger at a full gallop around the arena with Dad hanging on for dear life. Dad said that Trigger took off with such force that Dad's body must have looked like an unfurled flag, standing straight out, perpendicular to the ground. He made a complete loop around the stadium and out the door. Dad was so furious that he found a 2 × 4 and he lifted it up like a baseball bat. He started walking slowly and deliberately towards the horse and the Little Horse started backing up, with his head down, like a child who's ashamed of what he's done. He backed up against the wall and had nowhere to go. Dad said he swung the board back getting ready to hit that horse upside the head. But Little Trigger, in desperation, started going through every trick he knew. He blew kisses, he limped, he did everything but say to Dad, "I'm so cute, please don't beat me!" But when he sat back on his haunches and bowed his head in prayer—that did it for Dad. Just like his disagreements with Mom, Dad ended up doubled over with laughter, and so did the cowboys who witnessed this incredible scene.

Years after hearing this story, I saw a short, "Meet Roy Rogers," done by Republic in early 1941. It shows Dad and the Little Horse working on the same routine at Glenn's ranch. What a treasure!

Now, just because the Little Horse was a great performer of tricks doesn't mean that Old Trigger wasn't The Smartest Horse in the Movies—it just means that the Little Horse loved to get the attention. Whenever a director wanted a spectacular chase or stunt in the movies, that's when Old Trigger did his thing. In fact, in Dad's early movies the studio wouldn't rent a double for Trigger, so he did all of his own stunts.

Republic Director Billy Witney was probably Trigger's biggest fan, next to Dad. He loved to tell the story of when he got the idea to have Trigger jump fifty-gallon drums that were being rolled off the back of a truck Dad was chasing. The scene had originally called for Trigger to dodge the drums but Billy thought it would make the scene more exciting if Trigger jumped them. We were all up at Iverson's that day and I don't remember Dad questioning what Billy wanted Trigger to do. More surprising, neither did Glenn. Maybe they just thought Trigger could do anything. And, as it turns out, he could. They filmed that scene in one take. Then Billy sat down, turned white as a sheet and started shaking when he realized the danger he had placed Old Trigger in; he loved that horse. Over the many years I knew Billy, we were never together that he wouldn't tell me Trigger stories and he would always get tears in his eyes when speaking about Trigger's great heart and what an incredible athlete he was.

Another of his favorites had a scene that called for Dad to jump out of a second story window, run along the roof of the saloon, leap off the roof, run across the backs of two horses, then jump into Trigger's saddle. Of course, it wasn't Dad doing either stunt, it was Dad's stunt-double Joe Yrigoyen, but it was Old Trigger. Once Joe was in the saddle, he and Trigger would gallop down the street in pursuit of the bad guys.

Well, they walked through the scene once to get the timing and see how it would look. It was not a perfect rehearsal, but generally things worked okay and Trigger stood there and watched it all. The director shouted, "Let's shoot it." But now Trigger was wise to them. When he heard the word "action!" he turned his head and watched as Joe came running over the other horse. As soon as Joe leapt for Trigger's saddle . . . the horse started galloping away and Joe hit the dirt. They tried it a couple more times, and each time Trigger would wait for the last moment, then run off and leave Joe flying through the air toward nothing but ground.

Finally, Billy called a conference with Joe and others in the crew to try and figure out what to do. They couldn't just get another horse—this was a Roy Rogers picture and Trigger was the co-star! So they went to lunch and tried to come up with a plan. Billy decided that he wouldn't say "action;" he would simply give Joe a hand signal. They figured that if Trigger didn't hear the word, then naturally, he wouldn't know when to start running. So the cameras began to roll, Billy gave the silent signal, and Joe ran across the roof of the saloon, jumped down and ran across the two horses—meanwhile Trigger looked around him, saw what was happening, waited *just* long enough . . . and took off! Joe got just one foot in a stirrup and was hanging on for dear life as he and Trigger thundered down the street. Even without the words, you couldn't fool Trigger.

The third horse was Trigger Jr. He was a registered Tennessee Walker from Pennsylvania. They should have called him a "Tennessee Dancer." That horse was born to dance—he was Fred Astaire with four legs and he loved an audience. Boy, all you had to do was start his music, and Junior's neck would bow, his tail would go up, and he was ready—he absolutely loved to perform. He would dance and dance, and of course the crowds just loved him. Watching him perform, you could plainly see that he was having a great time. Besides that, he was beautiful. He was a darker palomino than Old Trigger and with the contrast of the dark gold with a snow white mane, blaze, tail, and four high white stockings, he was really flashy. It was always fun to watch Glenn train him and Dad rehearse and work with him at Glenn's place—but you had to see him in an arena. He was a totally different horse under the lights, with his music playing and a crowd applauding. I'm convinced that he *knew* just how good he looked.

Glenn Randall always kept a whole stable of palominos; that's why some people seem to believe that there were *lots* of Triggers, just as there have been many Lassies. In fact, one writer even claimed that there were forty-nine of them! That's nonsense. Dad owned the three that performed with him and then he owned a couple more that he used for breeding purposes. Dad never bred the Triggers because he took them to public events; he didn't want any problems with the stallions' behavior around other horses.

Glenn did have a circus Liberty act that used all palominos. A Liberty act is composed of horses that go around the ring in the circus without riders or harnesses. I suppose that, because he was so closely identified with Dad, whenever Glenn bought a palomino for the Liberty act, people automatically assumed the horse was going to become a new "Trigger." Actually, Dad worked the Liberty horses for two summers. Dad was the man in the middle with that long whip who put the horses through their paces. That's one act he had to rehearse over and over; it had a lot of cues—switches of direction, changes of order of the horses, and a lot of things to remember to get them to do what they were supposed to. It seems to me there were ten horses. In all the shows they did, I never saw those horses mess up. One of them, Elmer, made mistakes but it was all part of the act. They were incredible, beautifully trained animals, and Dad put them through their paces with skill and precision.

Dad got Trigger Jr. not to replace Trigger but as backup to the Little Horse, partly because the Little Horse gave Dad so many problems, but mainly because he was getting older. I don't remember Trigger Jr. making a movie other than, naturally enough, *Trigger Jr.* Dad didn't use him in the movies. But Dad did use specially trained palominos that were rented just for a particular stunt or sequence, if there was a fight scene. In the early 1950s, Trigger Jr. started doing the fairs and rodeos and the Little Horse was retired.

On *The Roy Rogers Show* and in several of their feature films together, Mom rode a horse named Buttermilk. He was Glenn Randall's champion roping horse. Dad and Glenn had looked for a horse that would look good next to Trigger. They tried Mom first on a really nice Paint, but the Paint was too flashy—at least Dad thought so. That one lasted a couple of movies. Then *I* got really lucky—they bought a beautiful palomino for Mom to ride that became my horse. He looked very much like Trigger, just smaller. He didn't do anything special, particularly; but he was a really nice, gentle gelding—a great horse. Mom rode him in one or two movies, but then Dad thought he looked too much like Trigger and they decided to keep looking. Dad gave him to me, and I named him Pal.

Then one day, Glenn brought his roping pony to the location so that he could train him between scenes. Somehow, the buckskin ended up being tied next to Trigger and somebody pointed out what an interesting combination they were: the large golden palomino and the small quarter horse with its light coat, black mane and tail and the black socks.

Mom tried him out. It was a good thing that Mom had taken riding lessons by then, because that horse was a handful. Being a roping pony he was really quick and could turn on a dime. Mom needed all of the skill she had acquired to be able to control him. But the most important thing was that the horses looked great together.

Mom and Dad were making *Utah* (1945) which, logically enough, was filmed up in Lone Pine, California. During a break in the filming, Mom and Buddy Sherwood, the wrangler on the film, were out looking at the sunset.

He turned to Mom and said, pointing at a beautiful milky sky, "Oh, doesn't that look like clabber?"

Mom replied, "You mean buttermilk?"

"Yeah," he said, "like clabber."

The buckskin's name was Soda, which Mom didn't really care for. Buddy's remark gave Mom an idea—she named her new pony Buttermilk Sky, but she always called him, simply, Buttermilk.

You have to admit, it could have been worse—he could have been named Clabber!

Dad bought Buttermilk from Glenn so that he would really be Mom's horse. Glenn immediately stopped using it as a roping horse and started training it to be compatible with Mom. He was a very smart horse. And fast! As soon as the clapper would go down on "action," they would take off. Being a quarter horse, he would often beat Trigger off the mark—and let me tell you, this was not a hit with Dad. He was always yelling, "Can't you control that horse?"

Dad was very protective of Trigger, but Trigger didn't hit his speed until after about five strides. Then he would blow the doors off any other horse. He just wasn't nearly as fast out the gate as Buttermilk was. If you look for it, you can see in their movies that Dad holds Trigger back a little bit in the chase scenes.

During one of the first interviews Mom did after Dad died, she told that story to the interviewer. She had never been able to tell it before, because Dad just wouldn't let her get through it—he would always interrupt her or correct her. But finally, she just couldn't wait to reveal that Buttermilk could beat Trigger. She was so proud of the fact but Dad would never admit it. To him, Trigger was the greatest horse ever, and nothing would ever prove him wrong.

As I said earlier, when we lived in Van Nuys, near Glenn Randall's place, I used to ride Trigger quite a bit. Because I wanted one of my own, Dad gave me Pal when he didn't work out for Mom.

I had ridden since I was a baby. I had trained Pal to move on voice command. I would say "trot" or "gallop" and he would do just that. I would say "stop" and he would stop. I only rode him with a rope halter and no saddle. He was a terrific, lovely horse and we worked together well; we were on the same wavelength somehow.

Dad saw how well I was doing with Pal and he told me Glenn had this really pretty little mustang that he thought I would like; his name was Tony. He was a pretty little bay gelding and he was "green broke," which means that the trainer has gotten the horse to the point where you can put a saddle and bridle on him and climb on his back without him pitching you into the cactus. A green broke horse isn't wild anymore, but he isn't even close to being trained. I don't know if Tony just wasn't very smart or if he was simply stubborn and intractable. We lived on five acres in Encino. Across the driveway from our house, we had a big pasture with a small herd of sheep, a couple of Black Angus cattle and some geese. In the rear part of the pasture stood a small copse of lilac trees. A long driveway meandered down to the back and made a big circle in front of the barn and the little cottage the foreman lived in. Then the road would double back on itself, come out of this circle and head back out to the street. Right in the middle of this circle was our "truck garden." We had a Swedish gardener named Gus Gustavson—he could grow anything. He spoke very broken English—but he was a very excitable older gentleman.

We kept the horses in the back pasture. Since Tony was only green broke, I had to ride him with a saddle. I didn't much care for that but it was a safety precaution that Dad absolutely insisted on. One afternoon, I made it my job to teach Tony to go forward. But after trying to get this idea across to him for about a couple of hours, he still wouldn't move . . . except to go backward. Dad hadn't been at the barn when I started working with Tony, but he came back about half of the way through.

He took one look and started laughing uproariously, He said, "Well, Sissy, it looks like you're in a fix!"

I said, more than a little angrily, "Well, I'm doing my best! He just won't listen."

Dad said, "You have to take control of him. Now, kick that horse and make him do what you say!"

Exasperated, I said, "Dad, do *you* want to ride him?"

So Dad mounted Tony and prepared to show me everything I was doing wrong. But Tony would only move backward for Dad, too. Before we knew what was happening, that stubborn horse was backing right through the truck garden, with Dad shouting at him to move forward. But he didn't listen to a word Dad had to say—and believe me, Dad had *plenty* to say on this occasion! Gus saw that Tony was tromping through the garden and he came running toward us, shouting—and, I suspect, swearing—in Swedish. I *know* that Dad was shouting and swearing in English. But that horse couldn't have cared less. Well, the next day it was back to Glenn's for Tony. I never saw him again.

That was about the only time I can remember that my Dad couldn't make an animal listen to reason—he could even get a *mountain lion* to make nice. Literally. Dad had once found a wounded mountain lion and had brought him home, put him in a cage and started nursing him back to health. If any of the rest of us came near that cat, he would scream and hiss like the wild animal he was. But when Dad would go over and talk to him, the mountain lion would practically purr like a kitten. Dad just had some kind of connection with every animal he ever met—well, except Tony.

I never had a relationship with an animal the way that Dad did. The communication that he could establish was unreal. He had a German shorthair named Sam. That dog was such a great yodeler that Dad once took him on *The Tonight Show* with Johnny Carson. Naturally, once he was there, Sam didn't yodel a single "ow-ooo." Luckily, my Dad had brought a tape of Sam performing and they played that while the camera zoomed in on Sam's placid face. It was hilarious. Not only could Sam yodel when he felt like it, but he could reason, too. My Dad could say almost anything to that dog and Sam knew what he was talking about; they really communicated.

He also had a pair of Russian boars. Dad had been hunting up around Santa Cruz with a bow and arrow on horseback. He killed a huge boar before he realized that "she" was the mother of two little piglets. So he brought these adorable little guys home with him and raised them at his ranch in Arroyo Grande. Every time these boars saw Dad, they would just go crazy—they seemed to adore him. They were big pigs, around 250 pounds, but they were like puppies around him; they roiled around his legs and squealed with glee. I don't know how you explain that kind of communication, but Dad was very definitely blessed with a gift for animals unlike that of almost anybody I've ever met.

As much as Dad loved Sam, I never saw him as attached to any other animal like he was to Old Trigger. Even, toward the end of his life, years after Trigger passed away, Dad would be going through the museum, and every time—*every time*—Dad got to the display where Trigger stands, he would tear up. How Dad loved that horse!

You, no doubt, have heard the story about Dad telling people that when he died, he wanted Mom to skin him out and place him in the museum on top of Trigger. Both Mom and Dad used different variations of that story in numerous interviews and talk shows over the past thirty-odd years. But what is interesting about it is that it had its origins in a heated discussion Mom and Dad had right after Trigger died.

Dad truly loved that horse easily as much as any other member of our family. He couldn't bear the thought of putting Trigger in the ground where he would be subject to the elements. He told Mom of his plans to have Trigger mounted and put on display so that all could share in his magnificence. Mom did not think much of the idea and told Dad it was wrong. Then she quoted the Bible verse that speaks of "dust to dust and ashes to ashes." Dad could not be dissuaded and a rather heated discussion ensued. It ended when Mom, in complete frustration, screamed at Dad, "Well, how would you like it if I had you stuffed when you died?" Dad replied in an instant, "That's all right, Honey. Just skin me out and put me up on Trigger, smiling and waving at the people." That put Mom away. She was beside herself with laughter and so ended another typical disagreement between my parents. Personally, I've never been sure that Dad was really kidding. He probably wouldn't have objected if she had done just that.

22

Paradise Cove

om bought a trailer on the beach at Paradise Cove shortly after she and Dad were married. It was her exclusive hideout and nobody was allowed to visit without an invitation—and that included Dad! She used the trailer as a retreat to get away, to read, write, reflect, and "recharge her batteries." Later, after Robin's death, it became the place where she wrote her books. Paradise Cove is a charming little inlet in the Malibu area. There was a bait shack, a hot dog stand, a fishing pier, and one of Malibu's best beaches—at least we thought so. You might have seen it in James Garner's TV series, *The Rockford Files*; it was the location they used for Rockford's residence/office.

Dad dearly loved to go deep sea fishing and he could launch his small fishing boat right off the dock. Since most of us suffered from seasickness, we would wait for his return and then barbeque whatever he caught. Mom's trailer was part of a mobile home park whose tenants tended to be predominantly retired people. In fact, I hardly remember seeing any other kids in the park—besides us and the one or two of our friends whom Mom would allow to visit occasionally.

When we *did* see other kids, they tended to be flocking around Smiley Burnette's trailer. Smiley—better known to Western movie fans as "Frog" Milhouse—was Gene Autry's former sidekick and a co-writer of many great songs. He was also the sidekick in *Under Western Stars* (1938), Dad's first starring role. Smiley had a trailer nearby, up on top of the bluff overlooking Paradise Cove. Sometimes when we were there on a weekend, he would invite us kids to one of his famous pancake breakfasts. There were always lots of kids there and I always thought they were Smiley's. But I recently found out that he only had a couple of kids, and it was *their* friends that made up the mob. Apparently, they were allowed to invite whoever they wanted—it made for a whole lot of kids, especially when our large family merged with them.

One Fourth of July, Dad and Mom had invited a couple of other families to join us, and we all took our food and boxes of fireworks to the cove for a typical Independence Day celebration. We spent the day swimming and frolicking in the ocean, and then Dad made a bonfire where everyone roasted hot dogs and marshmallows. We older kids were told to clean up the younger ones after supper while the adults put everything back in the cars in anticipation of the evening's entertainment. There must have been four boxes—the giant assortments—of fireworks in a big stack and we kids couldn't wait for what we knew would be the best show ever! We had already been there for a full day so everybody was getting pretty rambunctious. We were all wired with impatient anticipation and it seemed as if the sun would never set. Dad was waiting for the perfect moment. In the meantime, he passed out sparklers to all of the kids to keep us quiet until it got dark enough to really do a proper job with the fireworks. It was a good thought and probably would have gone as planned, except for one small hitch—some of the smaller kids really weren't all that careful with the sparklers. Especially Dusty, who was only about four years old at the time. Can you see where this story is going?

Dusty was an inquisitive kid and he decided that he'd like to take a look at these fireworks that he'd heard so much about. Using the sparkler to light his way, Dusty went to peek under the lid of the top box and, while doing so, he tripped in the sand, dropped his sparkler into the box and KA-BOOM! I must say, it was the most spectacular display of fireworks we had ever seen. With four packed boxes of assorted fireworks, there were rockets shooting in every direction, pinwheels rolling along the sand, sparks shooting out of numerous boxes of sparklers, lots of small explosions from the firecrackers—and lots of kids and adults scattering for their lives! The other tenants of Paradise Cove later remarked that they had never seen such a sight. Well, neither had any of us. It was an amazing show, but a disappointingly short one—it was all over in a matter of minutes, instead of the two hours as originally planned. All that was left were black ashes from the "snakes" and twisted metal from the sparklers. I think Dad was more disappointed than any of us. He was as big if not a bigger kid than any of us and he had been looking forward to this evening for weeks, probably more than us. He had planned just how he was going to stake the pinwheels, and in what order they were going to send up the rockets. Now, it was all over, literally in a flash.

Poor Dusty! Dad hollered, Mom fussed, and we older kids were *furious* that our evening's entertainment was cut short. We ragged on that poor kid for days afterward. In fact, I don't think we've ever stopped teasing him about it. Very luckily, nobody got hurt, nobody got burned. It's just that it all went up at once. After that, anytime we were going to do fireworks, Dad always kept Dusty as far away from the cache of fireworks as possible.

23

Grief and Acceptance

*I*n many ways, our family lived privileged lives. We were given opportunities that lots of people don't have, enjoyed countless wonderful experiences and met great people in myriad walks of life. But we also endured more than our share of heartbreak and tragedy—not once, but again and again. Mom and Dad had to face the loss of three of their children, Sandy, Debbie, and Robin, their only child together. How they survived those tragedies—and how they helped the rest of us through those terrible times—says a lot about what kind of people Mom and Dad were, and how strong was their faith in God and in the healing power of family.

Everyone adored my sister Debbie. She was a very bright, outgoing, sunny young lady—always an achiever. During the four years before Debbie came to us, her life had been harsh and frightening. She had been provided with barely enough food and little, if any, love or attention. Maybe it was because of this rough start that she turned out to be such a generous and kind soul.

The family was now living in the farthest corner of the San Fernando Valley, in Chatsworth. After Linda, Mimi, and I married and moved away, Mom and Dad joined a new church, Chapel in the Canyon. Two or three times a year the youth groups at the church would take toiletries, clothing, toys, and other necessities down to an orphanage in Mexico. The boys had gone on several of these trips but they had their first summer jobs, digging trenches for a builder, and couldn't make the next trip. However, the girls were eligible for the first time; they were now preteens. Dodie came down with the flu the day before their scheduled trip. Mom was going to keep them both home. The boys had always gone together and she wanted the girls to travel together, especially on their first trip. Debbie pleaded and begged. Her whole Sunday school class was going and she told Mom she didn't think it was fair she had to stay home just because Dodie was sick. Mom didn't want to seem unreasonable, so she finally consented to let Debbie go on the trip.

Debbie was extremely gregarious and full of life; she could never sit still. She and her closest girlfriend were standing up in front of the bus talking and visiting with their friends. The minister later said that he had asked them to sit down several times, which they did—for a moment. Then they would bounce back up again. She was once again standing up in the front when the bus blew a tire, swerved into the median strip and hit a car coming from the opposite direction, head-on. Several people were injured in the accident but only two were killed—Debbie and her girlfriend. The year was 1964.

I heard about the accident on the TV at my in-laws' home in San Jose where the kids and I had just arrived for a visit. My husband, Bill, had dropped us off on his way to a job in Marin County and it would be a couple of hours before I could reach him by phone. The TV hadn't said that one of my siblings was dead, only that there were fatalities from the crash of the Chapel in the Canyon bus. I knew in my heart that one of the kids was dead, but I thought it was one of my brothers. It never occurred to me that one of the girls would be on that trip, since they had never gone before. I grabbed the telephone and called the house again and again but I couldn't get through. That's when I knew for sure that something was terribly wrong. I got through to Bill, who immediately started back to pick us up. Then, finally, I reached Mom at the house. When she told me that it was Debbie, I was stunned—it just wasn't possible. Mom was sobbing and I felt so helpless, stranded hours away from her. I told her I would get there as quickly as I could.

Bill got to his folks around midnight and we tried to get a couple hours of rest. However, I didn't sleep at all and we were up before sunrise and practically raced back to the Valley. I found a friend to watch my own kids and arrived at the house by mid-afternoon. My friend Judy was there helping Mom make arrangements for Debbie's body to be transported to Los Angeles for the funeral. Mom immediately gave me my assignments: man the phones and locate Tom and Barbara, who had just left for vacation in their trailer.

Mom was facing this crisis without Dad by her side. Dad had just been transferred to Bel Air Sanitarium where he had been fighting a life-threatening staph infection. He picked the infection up at the hospital where he had undergone spinal surgery a couple of weeks before and was transferred when he wasn't getting better at the hospital. The doctors had told us only a couple of days before that he was finally starting to recover. Now Mom was faced with how to tell Dad about Debbie's death. The doctors told Mom that this news could be a major setback for Dad and suggested Mom try to keep the news from him until he was stronger. Mom instructed everyone not to get Dad upset when we visited. We should put on happy faces and talk about the weather. She arranged for there to be no newspapers and for the TV in his room to be conveniently broken. Mom insisted to the doctors that she wanted to be the one to tell him as soon as they thought he was strong enough to take the news. Then one of Dad's "dear friends" went and told him—he didn't even check with Mom. The news just about killed Dad! He was beside himself with grief and because he couldn't help Mom due to the infection and his continuing weakness. How could they console each other, when they were so many miles apart?

The driveway was blocked by cars coming and going. It seemed as though everyone in the Valley wanted to personally offer Mom their help and support. It never seemed to occur to any of them that she wouldn't have time to visit with them; they just wanted to tell her how sorry they were. By the time we got through the funeral, I had been without sleep for three days. I wasn't able to locate Tom and Barbara until after the services, but

I had talked to every highway department, most of the sheriff's departments, and several police departments along their vacation route.

As soon as Dad was better and had returned home, he started looking for a place to move. He told Mom that he saw Debbie's face in every room of the house and that he felt they needed a change to heal from their grief. They soon relocated to Apple Valley.

The summer of Debbie's death, Sandy started pressing Mom and Dad to allow him to enlist. He had been fascinated with the art of soldiering since he first came to us. When they were little guys, the bedroom he shared with Dusty had Confederate and Union soldiers set up on every surface. The Stars and Bars always hung on their wall in a place of honor. Sandy, because of the treatment he received before he joined us, had always had a difficult time in school, but he was our authority on the Civil War. He told Mom and Dad that he knew he wasn't college material and that he wanted to get started on what he hoped would be his career. Then he promised them he would earn his G.E.D. while in the service, if they would only let him join the Army.

I've always thought they agreed to let him enlist because they didn't think he would pass the physical. I think they were sure he would be turned down. They seemed to be amazed when Sandy told them he had been accepted and would soon leave for boot camp. Sandy was already in the Army when Mom, Dad, Dusty, and Dodie moved to Apple Valley.

Once again, I think that Mom and Dad had figured that he wouldn't get through boot camp, but they didn't realize just how determined he was. When he became a private, they became concerned about where he would be stationed. Sandy wanted to go to Vietnam where a lot of his friends already were. Mom and Dad prayed that the Army would realize that he was not physically fit to see combat. Their prayers were answered and Sandy was placed in a tank unit that was sent to Germany. Just before going overseas, Sandy and his girlfriend, Sharon, announced their engagement and everyone was happy that Sandy was realizing his dreams.

It was Halloween morning when I got a call from Dusty saying that Dad had just been notified that Sandy was dead. They didn't have many details yet but it appeared that he had died while in the base hospital. Mom was going to be returning that day from visiting Grandma Smith in Texas—it was Mom's birthday—and she was expected to arrive at Los Angeles Airport shortly. Since he and Dad couldn't make it to Los Angeles in time to meet her plane, he asked me if I could get to the airport in time, in case the press broke the story before Mom got back to Apple Valley. It was barely a year since Debbie's death and we knew the press would be all over us.

I called my sister Mimi to go with me, then called United Airlines and asked them to have a room set aside for our use. Then we took off for the airport. It turns out that I had made a mistake in asking Mimi to accompany me. Bless her heart, Mom took one look at Mimi's devastated face and immediately jumped to the conclusion that something terrible had happened to Dad. She started asking me if he was going to be all right, where he was, how soon we could get to him. I assured her that Dad was fine but that I did indeed have bad news. As gently as possibly, I told her that Sandy was dead. I was really worried about her. She had very high blood pressure and I was worried that this news, combined with all the trauma of the previous year, would give her a heart attack and we would lose her. Anticipating this, I had even tried to get her doctor to meet us at LAX, but he couldn't. We were just getting her to United's offices, when she spotted Dad and Dusty coming down the ramp corridor towards us.

By then Dusty had talked to Germany and had more details about what had occurred. Sandy had received a promotion the previous day and set off to celebrate with a couple of his buddies at the Enlisted Men's Club. Some older guys dared him to celebrate with a drink that contained a little bit of every liquid that was behind the bar. This potent concoction made him violently ill. One of his buddies took him to the base infirmary. He was supposed to simply sleep it off, but the next morning they found him dead. He had gotten sick again during the night and choked to death.

This new tragedy was devastating to Mom and Dad. They had been so concerned about Sandy being sent into combat and now they had lost him, at nineteen, to a stupid dare. We left the airport for the long trip to Apple Valley.

Although Mom and Dad had only recently moved into their new home and joined a new church, Church of the Valley Presbyterian, the people of Apple Valley were wonderful to them. Mom and Dad's new minister, Bill Hansen, arrived at the house only minutes after we did. Their new friends and neighbors began arriving with food, flowers, and expressions of concern, which they left by the door. Many of the expressions of concern said that if Mom or Dad needed anything, they had only to call and then provided a telephone number. After the circus we had been put through in Encino and Chatsworth, I was amazed at what a wonderful community this was.

Shortly after Sandy's death, Mom and Dad made the decision to entertain our troops in Vietnam. They put together a group of entertainers and spent two weeks in the country they had prayed that Sandy would not be sent to.

I don't know how they survived losing three children. Well, yes, I do. It was directly through their faith that they were able to go on. I don't remember Mom going to a psychologist or even a counselor. Of course she did talk to her minister and a couple of her other close friends—who also happened to be ministers. Mom's writing was a wonderful outlet for her. I think it enabled her to deal with her feelings; putting them down on paper helped her work through a lot of her grief.

A few years later, I was to learn first-hand exactly what my poor mother had gone through when I lost my son Mark. His death made no sense to me. He and his wife, Shawna, were so happy. They had two little boys, two-year-old Sterling McKay and their brand-new son, Ashton. You never saw a more handsome or happy family. Mark had raced bicycles, motorcycles, and cars since he was a kid. Now he was editor and publisher of *Off Road* magazine. He was in a sport that had a good safety record, and yet he was gone. He died in an instant.

Mark raced whenever he could, but he didn't usually tell me what he was doing until afterward. I just couldn't stand the thought of the risks he was taking. One weekend, he and Shawna joined the rest of the Rogers clan at a dinner honoring Mom and Dad that was hosted by their church in Apple Valley. This was their chance to introduce their brand-new baby, Ashton, to the family and for Sterling to get reacquainted with his cousins. All the children and grandchildren were here, lots of pictures were taken—it was a huge, wonderful event.

The following Wednesday morning, I was surprised to get a call from Mark. He said, "Mom I just wanted you to know that I am going to Wisconsin on assignment but I'm not racing." I told him that I was glad he called. I said I was sure that Shawna was relieved that he wasn't racing and that he should have a good time. The odd thing is, he had *never* called me before like that. He only let me know about his races after the fact. I thought the phone call was very strange but I thought no more about it until I got the call from Todd, his step-brother, on Saturday morning that Mark had been killed.

When I got that terrible call, I remember that I couldn't get my breath. Everything was a horrible, foggy blur. It hurt too much to think or feel, so I just refused to deal with it. I went through the motions, attended the services and it wasn't until a week later, after family and friends had returned to their homes, that I allowed myself to even grieve. Without Larry's strength and quiet support, I don't know that I could have even gone through the motions. In fact, it's only now while putting this down on paper, that I am starting to remember what happened that awful day and the days following. Of course, I have to ask Larry about a lot of it, since I totally blocked it out until now. I am really upset with myself that I was no help to my daughter-in-law during that dreadful time, but I was absolutely unable to cope and just shut down.

Our daughter Kerry was at our condo when I took the call from Mark's stepbrother Todd. I don't think that I was able to do anything but keep saying, "No . . . no . . ." Kerry told Larry that she thought Mark had been killed and then Larry did my job. He notified Mom and, although she and Dad were already in their late seventies, she said they were coming to us right away. Larry said that he tried to dissuade her but she told him that I had always been there for her, and they were coming. Then he went about calling the rest of the family.

Within a couple of hours Mom and Dad arrived at our condo in Port Hueneme. My sister Mimi was helping out and my half sister and her husband were flying in from Texas. That, I guess, is the most comforting thing of all. In good times and hard times, your family is there to share it with you. We might fight and have disagreements under everyday conditions, and we definitely lead separate lives on a regular basis, but when something bad happens, everyone is right there. And that is one of life's greatest blessings.

Poor Dad, he never knew what to do in a situation like this. He would give your arm a pat or hug your shoulders. He once told me that he finally got to the point where he decided we're never going to understand why awful things happen until we're gone, then the Lord would explain it to us. But until the Lord did, Dad was not even going to try. I think that's how he got through the bad times, waiting for the Lord's explanation.

Sometimes that's all we can do—life gives us so many puzzling questions. When Mark's car crashed, he died in an instant and the driver of the car was barely hurt at all. They put him in the hospital with a couple of scrapes and scratches but he was fine. Six months later—almost to the day—he died in a hit-and-run. What can you learn from something like that except, when it's your time, it's your time?

After Mark's death I, like everybody, looked for somebody to blame or something that should have been done. But the truth is, nothing could have been done. They were way out in the middle of nowhere in an off-road area. Mark had died instantly. So even if there had been a hospital next door it wouldn't have made any difference. Sandy died in a hospital; he choked to death because he had gotten sick to his stomach, something that had been going on from the time he was a little boy. How could it have been prevented?

I can't fault Dad for how he dealt with tragedy because I believe you have to find what works for you in order to continue. Like Daddy, I figure that maybe someday we will understand, but for the moment whatever God wills is what is going to happen. The only thing I know how to do is just go with the flow; I don't know what else to do.

Dad depended on Mom knowing the right things to say and do in the here and now and, thank the Lord, she did. She later told Larry that I had kept asking her, over and over, why she hadn't told me before how badly it hurt. She had, of course, several times—I just hadn't understood until I lost my own child. Mom even did the eulogy at Mark's funeral service—how, I have no idea. She was an incredible lady with an incredible faith and total trust in her Lord.

Dad, however, came up with the best solution to get through the days following Mark's death. A couple of months later Dad called and asked me to go to work at the museum. This was a whole new world and I embraced it wholeheartedly. I joined the national and state museum associations; I took classes on how to promote nonprofits. I threw myself totally into this new experience and pretty much cut myself off from everything else. But at least I was functioning. I now know about the catharsis of getting it all down on paper. Where I have been unable or unwilling to deal with the loss of Mark, having to think about that time and ask Larry about the details and sequence of events, is finally allowing me to face what happened and come to terms with it. No wonder Mom tried to do this as soon after her loss as possible. I have always been a slow learner when compared with her.

24

Happy Trails

*M*om and Dad were genuine superstars. They made movies; they released hit records; and they headlined at countless stage shows, rodeos, state fairs, and other public appearances. Their television series, *The Roy Rogers Show,* was broadcast in first-run episodes from 1952 until 1957, then went into worldwide syndication. It continued to delight kids in the United States on Saturday mornings until 1964. Somewhere in the world, it is still being shown today.

After their own show went off the air, they regularly appeared on nearly every musical or variety show on television—*The Dinah Shore Show, The Nashville Palace, The Kraft Music Hall,* to mention just a few. They appeared with the Statler Brothers, Barbara Mandrell, Andy Williams, Dean Martin. And on whichever show they appeared, that series registered some of its highest ratings of the season.

In 1962, officials at ABC decided that Mom and Dad should have their own variety show. It was called *The Roy Rogers and Dale Evans Show.* In addition to co-stars who were already identified with Mom and Dad—like Pat Brady and the Sons of the Pioneers—the series featured folksy comedian Cliff Arquette (as Charley Weaver), folksinger Kathy Taylor, and the Ralph Carmichael Orchestra. Ralph Carmichael was already making his name as one of the leading lights in Christian music, and he and Mom, especially, worked together often.

In addition to music and comedy, *The Roy Rogers and Dale Evans Show* featured trick horses and rodeo and circus acts. All that was fine with the network, but other parts of the show weren't. Mom and Dad insisted that the end of every program would feature a salute to God and country. The executives at ABC were less than thrilled with that, apparently feeling that they would offend viewers who didn't share Mom and Dad's religious and political points of view. Mom and Dad were also very involved at that time with the fight against world communism.

What was unusual about the show is that Mom and Dad, with the help of Art Rush, had sold all the commercials that supported it. They, not ABC, had signed all their own sponsors. They had many advertisers committed for a full season. But ABC had threatened to pull the plug if Mom and Dad continued to end the show with their religious and patriotic medley. Mom and Dad didn't believe ABC was serious. But they were. After only two months, the network took it off the air. The last episode aired on December 29, 1962.

Mom and Dad were stunned; they couldn't believe that ABC had made such an arbitrary decision—especially on a money-making show! They never had their own series again, although they remained popular guests on other people's shows virtually until the ends of their lives.

Even though their show business careers slowed down considerably as they aged, Mom and Dad never lost their faithful audience. They were both very moved to have received the prestigious Golden Boot Award, annually given by the Motion Picture & Television Fund Foundation to the finest Western performers in history. Mom and Dad were among the first recipients. Dad received the Founders Award from the same organization for his lifetime achievement in Western films.

After Dad died, the Golden Boot committee voted Mom the Founders Award, in recognition of her body of work. Here again, she was a trailblazer—the first woman to receive this honor. But when I told Mom the thrilling news, she didn't quite get it. Why were they giving her the Founders Award, she wanted to know? "I didn't found it," Mom insisted. "Pat Buttram founded the Golden Boot!"

It took me weeks of constant reinforcement that this award was for her entire career and because she changed women's roles in Westerns. Up until Mom, most women in Westerns tended to be there just so they could get menaced by the bad guy and rescued by the good guy. They hardly ever had more than twenty-five or thirty lines to say in the whole movie. But Mom was different. All of a sudden, here was a woman who was a true co-star with the hero, a woman who could hold her own, who could outthink everybody else in the film and, if push came to shove, could rescue herself. I kept reminding her of all this and she finally gave in and started working on her acceptance speech.

Even so, Mom could be unpredictable and I warned them at the Boot that she might accept the award and she might not.

When the big night came on Saturday, August 11, 2000, she was in fine spirits. For years, Mom had always said grace before the Golden Boot banquet and so, naturally, we asked her to say grace this year, too. She was in her wheelchair and the microphone was handed to her as she sat at her table. Everyone bowed their heads—and Mom launched into . . . her acceptance speech. She and I had been working so hard on it, that she was ready to go! She was getting to the part where she first saw Gabby Hayes and she knew that she was actually in Hollywood.

I crept up beside Mom—I was seated a couple of tables away— and gently reminded her that she was supposed to be saying grace. She told me she would say grace when she was ready! I softly repeated that she would accept her award later. So, she said a sentence or two of grace—but I had done such a good job in getting her to memorize her acceptance speech, that she segued right back into it.

I had to interrupt her a second time. This time she asked the guests if they were really so hungry that she couldn't say her piece? I thought the audience was going to lynch me. Afterward I kept hearing, "Why did you do that? We would have listened to her all night." I said, "Yes, you would have—you *definitely* would have been here all night!" She was on a roll.

Bless her, Mom must have felt it was going to be her last time in front of this audience, and it was. But she was feisty right up until the end and, as always, totally in charge.

I think what Dad hated most about getting old was the feeling of having to depend on others. One of the things that really got to him in the later years was his bad back. He had to have a spinal fusion just before Debbie's death; the doctors had fused his top three vertebrae. He learned that a lot of that trouble came from all of those fight scenes he had done in the movies. Now, as you probably know, people don't *really* hit each other when they're fighting in the movies. They throw a punch that goes right past the opponent's head and, through the camera angle and the sound effects, it looks genuine—and painful. Oddly enough, it was that very act—throwing a punch but not connecting with anything— that had caused problems for Dad. It's an unnatural motion, all that outward thrust and no recoil. It slowly wore away the cushioning. At the end, all of his joints were bone on bone. He was so incredibly physical all his life that he simply wore everything out.

Of course, part of his back problem was congenital. Dusty tried to enlist in the Air Force when he was in high school. But when he went for his physical, they found that he had the same condition as Dad—a narrowing of the spine. That condition, in addition to the very active life Dad led, eventually worked together to give him some serious problems.

For years he lived with awful, constant pain. It finally got to the point where he couldn't get out of bed. If I was staying at the house, I would take him coffee in the morning. In order to sit up, he would try to brace his head with both hands and then roll out of bed without having to move his neck. If he wasn't successful and his neck moved, which usually happened, he would just start screaming; that went on for ages before he agreed to undergo surgery.

He finally went to UCLA and underwent the spinal fusion. It wasn't like it is now where they go in through the throat which is a lot less traumatic and the healing time is less; they had to split his back open. It left his neck very stiff. He could turn his head but not move it from side to side.

My husband, Larry, turned out to be a Godsend in the last years of Mom and Dad's life. I don't know what I would have done without him. I can't imagine anyone else being able to step into a situation like that and be able to handle it with such patience and good humor.

Larry and I originally moved to Victorville to work at the museum. But we had only been there a short time when Mom had a stroke—she'd had a heart attack a year earlier. Dad was having health problems, but that had been going on for a very long time. However, shortly after we moved to Apple Valley, Dad lost his driver's license and was no longer mobile. So Larry became his driver and was with him almost every day. Dad wouldn't let Dusty or me drive him around. When he lost his license he was very depressed. I understood his feelings—the loss of control and autonomy—but the fact was that he was a *horrible* driver. He just couldn't see. He had lost part of the vision in his left eye due to a ministroke in his eye that doctors call the "drawn blind syndrome." A piece of plaque breaks away from the wall of an artery, works its way behind an eye, and you lose vision in the top of that eye. It's an indicator that you are about to have a major stroke.

It happened to him when he was on the set of the TV series *The Fall Guy*. Dad was guest-starring in an episode called, appropriately enough, "Happy Trails." When he first started he had trouble with his vision, he had no idea what it was; he just thought he had something in his eye, it cleared up, and he didn't tell anybody what happened. The next day, driving to location at Vasquez Rocks, it happened again—a shadow across part of his eye—but this time he had a terrible headache as well. He mentioned to the nurse on the set that he had a bad headache and he asked her for an aspirin, but he didn't tell her his symptoms.

Larry and I visited the set later that afternoon. Dad told us about this headache that he couldn't seem to get rid of and that he was having trouble seeing out of his right eye, but he told us not to tell Mom there was anything wrong. I said we wouldn't if he would go to the eye doctor immediately, and he agreed.

But by the time Dad finally got around to going to the doctor it was a couple of days later and Mom had returned. The doctor took one look at Dad's eye and said, "Go to your cardiologist right now. Do not go home to pack or anything. Get in the car and go to your heart doctor right now!" Dad called Mom and

Mom called ahead to Dad's doctor and told him what the eye doctor had said. She and I drove together while Larry rode with Dad and we all met Dad's doctor at UCLA. That's when they found out that he was in real trouble: both carotid arteries were blocked and needed immediate surgery. Ten days later there would be a second surgery to unblock the second artery.

Larry and I weren't living in Apple Valley at that time; we were just visiting. So it was Larry who drove him down for the second surgery. It was because of his blocked arteries that this plaque had lodged behind his eye and impaired his vision. There was nothing that could be done; his loss of vision was permanent. In addition, this blood clot would probably expand slightly with the passage of time.

By the time we moved to Apple Valley in 1994, he was starting to have additional problems with his good eye. Dad was starting to develop what the doctor called a "floating" cataract. His vision would go in and out on his good eye. Sometimes, he could still go shooting and hit everything he aimed at. At other times, he couldn't see anything clearly.

About a year after we moved to Apple Valley it was time for Dad to get his license renewed. We made the appointment, Dusty went with him, and Dad flunked every part of the test: the written exam, the eye exam, and the driving part. In fact, Dad pulled out in front of another car before he and the examiner sitting next to him had even left the DMV parking lot, and the examiner had to grab the wheel. Finally, Dad gave up his license, albeit reluctantly.

When Mom stopped driving after her stroke, it didn't seem to bother her to be driven. In fact, I think she rather enjoyed it. But it bothered Dad, and he didn't like any of us doing it. We were his kids and *he had always driven us*. For some reason, though, he would let Larry drive him around. Larry would come over to the house and say, "Hey, do you want to go play today?" Larry would joke with him and put it on a lighter kind of basis. Larry would often ask Dad to ride along on errands, and Dad would go with him. Maybe Larry chose to take that tack with Dad because before he ended up with a business degree, he studied to be a coach. He would have been terrific at it—he's a great motivator. But however he managed it, Larry could get Dad to do things that the rest of us just couldn't. Or to put it another way, Dad would allow Larry to do things for him that he wouldn't let his own kids do for him.

It's also possible that because Larry wasn't one of his "kids," Dad felt a little more comfortable showing his weakness. Maybe it's like when he would visit kids in the hospital that he didn't know—but he wouldn't visit *us* in the hospital! In his mind, we were his kids and he was never going to depend on us. I know that having to depend on me to do his meds and other caregiving needs was almost more than he could take.

There were times when Dad would be furious with me. The doctor didn't want him wearing his boots because he was having a hard time with his balance, so one time while he was in the hospital, we took all of his boots and put them out in an outside wardrobe. I told Mom that we were just not going to discuss the boot thing with Dad because we knew it was going to become a big issue. Mom agreed that it was for Dad's welfare. Well, Dad got home from the hospital and it took him about two days before he was on his feet. The first thing he said was, "Where are my boots?" Mom said, "Cheryl put them in the outside closet." She sold me out in an instant! I got an immediate phone call from Dad, and he was livid.

"I've been wearing boots all my life!"

I said, "No, you haven't—you used to wear tennis shoes at home."

"Well I'm going to wear boots now!" And he did, right up to the end of his life.

It's got to be tough as you age and the tables get turned. I know it was really difficult for both of them. Mom had so many diet restrictions and it was up to me to keep foods away from her that the doctor said she absolutely could not have because she had heart problems and was a diabetic. That was tough. It was hard on her because she had always been in charge, and it was hard on me to make sure that it at least *seemed* that she was still in charge. There were many times that we butted heads.

Interestingly, it was never difficult to make them take their medicine. They were actors. They had been trained from the get-go, that in Hollywood, you keep the weight off to look good in front of the cameras and you sleep when it's convenient. So they were used to diet pills and sleeping pills, the whole Hollywood thing that everyone's read about for years. Mom stopped taking the diet pills as soon as she was no longer making films. Not Dad—he always took sleeping pills. When I moved up to Victorville, I got him to stop taking them because by that time, with his heart problems, they were too dangerous. It took about four or five months to get him weaned off that stuff. But he was still on his scale two or three times a day—it was just habit, the habit of years. Thank heavens he never had a problem with his weight. He wasn't a real healthful eater, and I don't think he ever had been. In fact, he was a junk food junkie: he loved ice cream, pancakes, eggs, bacon, and all kinds of desserts. He would eat breakfast three times a day, if he could.

Toward the end, he wouldn't eat much of anything at all. The doctors were so worried that they urged Mom to let him eat whatever he wanted—no matter what it was. But if he asked for eggs, Mom would say, "Oh, but you're not supposed to have eggs."

I would have to say, "Yes, Mom, the doctor said he can have them."

Mom would reply, "But they're not good for him!" It was really hard to convince her that anything we could get in him was good for him at that point. She had been watching out for him for so long, and those habits were imbedded so deep within her that she couldn't grasp that the doctor was allowing, and even encouraging, him to do things now that had previously been limited to once a week.

But even though he often felt bad, Dad never lost his sense of fun; he was a teenager throughout his entire life. You never had to worry about Dad being dignified in private because that was just not going to happen. Dad never got over the fact that he was in Hollywood and getting paid to do things that were so much fun. And he was energized by his fans.

His museum is what kept him going those last years; being able to go to the museum often got him out of bed. Dad would go there and the visitors couldn't believe they were seeing the *real* Roy Rogers! They would tell him about the effect he had on them as kids. So many of them, like Larry, had lost their dads in the war. There were others whose dads were in prison or were alcoholics or just weren't good dads. So many, many people told Dad that he was the one who kept them on the straight and narrow; and now they were teachers, cops, doctors, ministers. He heard those stories every day. Who *wouldn't* love hearing things like that? That's what kept him going for so long.

I think he enjoyed most of his life. If it hadn't gotten to where it was so physically painful for him, I believe that he would have kept going even longer.

His fans were so loyal to him precisely because he *was* a true role model. He built up a real relationship with them. They believed that they knew his real character—and they did. Dad was as much of a straight-shooter off the screen as on. In the early days of his career he was often offered other kinds of movie roles. As much as he might have enjoyed playing a villain—and I believe he was a good enough actor to have carried it off—Dad always refused. He said he didn't want to confuse little kids, by being a good guy in one movie and bad guy in another. He really liked being Roy Rogers.

I never thought he was an actor when I was a kid. It wasn't until he did the 1975 feature film *Mackintosh and T.J.* that it dawned on me that he could act. In fact, he was really good. He was always so natural and effortless that I made the common mistake of believing that he was "playing himself." But look at his first movie, *Under Western Stars*. In it he plays the part of a young man running for Congress and everybody breaks into song all the time—it's definitely not realism in any way. Yet he is so believable, so honest on screen. Like many of the greats, part of his gift was in making it look as if he wasn't "acting" but was just going along, being himself. "Roy Rogers" is exactly who Dad really was. Maybe that's why we never drew much of a line between the two.

When Sandy had only been with us for a few months, he and Dusty were watching *The Roy Rogers Show* and Dad happened to pass through the den. Sandy hollered at Dad, "Hey, Dad, look! There's Roy Rogers!"

I remember watching Dad go through a script, marking out or changing lines. "Roy wouldn't say this," he'd say, or, "Roy would never do that." And then he would write in what Roy *would* do.

Dad, Mom, and I attended a rough-cut screening of *Mackintosh and T.J.* By a weird coincidence, the editing had been done at CBS Television Studios, which meant that we were back at Republic again. I sat in the viewing room watching this movie about an over-the-hill cowboy who has lost his wife and son and meets up with a little kid, and I was very moved by it. I turned to Mom and said—and I must have had a note of surprise in my voice— "My God, he is a *good* actor!" And I heard Dad say in this little voice on the other side of Mom, "Well, I learned something in all those years." I felt about an inch high.

Mom and Dad were great role models. Neither of them started out to be that; it's not something that anyone sets out on a career path to be. With Dad it was a decision that he made once he became Roy Rogers, the hero, he was going to be a good guy in his private life as well as his professional life. Luckily for him, it was during an era, and he was at the right studio, where he could do that—build up and develop a single character, and make it the focus of an entire career. I don't think that most actors have that luxury; they are just out there scrambling for whatever part they can get.

In Mom's case it was really through her books that her influence was most felt, more than the roles that she played. That's too bad in a way, because the roles that she played were wonderful—a strong, intelligent career woman, to Dad's dumb cowboy hero. Bless his heart, he was the hero, but it would take him a whole movie to figure out what was going on most of the time. It was through her books that Mom was able to help people, and through her Christian testimony. Just living through the things she did and coming through them with such grace set a path for others to follow. I don't remember her losing her dignity through any of the horrible things she went through, and all of her tragedies were so public.

While Dad adored coming to the museum and meeting his fans, Mom preferred working on her *next* project. When she had a new book come out, she would agree to do a signing. But Mom didn't live in the past. To her, that was looking backward and she always wanted to look forward. She really had no interest in talking about her career or going down memory lane in any way. To her, it was always, "What's next?"

As I said earlier, Mom put everything in her twenty-nine books. She wrote about her past husbands, her band days, everything. I think that she reasoned that in Hollywood, eventually, everything becomes fodder for the reporters or the fans that need to know every detail of their favorite actors' lives. She figured if people wanted to know about her, they might as well hear the truth, from the horse's mouth. Dad, however, kept his own counsel.

Another of the questions I'm asked a lot is, "What is the best advice your Mother ever gave you?" That's easy. She told us to live each and every day as though it's the last one we'll ever have. In other words, you don't want to end up in front of St. Peter saying, "Oops!" I think that is great advice and I passed it along to my kids and grandkids.

Even though we grew up with little or no privacy and, even though this was not a choice we made but rather the result of a choice our parents made, it wasn't all bad. There were some wonderful benefits. I have met some of the most famous people in the world without being in the spotlight myself. I wouldn't be doing what I do now for the museum and with the Motion Picture and Television Fund if my parents had not been Roy and Dale. We knew for two weeks that Dad was getting weaker and weaker and that his time with us was drawing to a close. Suddenly he seemed to be free of the pain that had racked his body for so long. He was almost serene. He told jokes, sang, and yodeled up to his last day. He also talked to Grampy and assured us that Grampy had said that everything was going to be fine and that we shouldn't worry. We all wished him a good night, he went to sleep, and we left him with his night nurse. He slipped away about 4:00 A.M. with just a little sigh. The nurse wasn't even sure at first that he was gone.

The day of Dad's funeral was the day from hell. We had three services for him. Originally the family was only to attend the services in the afternoon. But Mom decided we would go to all of them, which, of course, is what we did. There was a public service in the morning at the church. They needed a couple of hours to clear people out of the church and then to allow others back in for the friends-and-family service. In the middle of that service the family left for the private graveside services. Then we returned to the church to greet those friends and extended family members who had stuck around. The whole day was taken up with this. Thousands of people attended; it was incredible and awesome.

The drive to the cemetery was almost spooky. I've spoken about how Dad communicated with animals. All along the route that we traveled from the church to the cemetery, people were standing in front of their homes, sort of paying homage as Dad took his final trip. But what was weird, is that the dogs along the route were also standing along the road, watching, almost at attention. It was very eerie.

Mom got through it all, as sick as she was. She was in a wheelchair after the heart attack and strokes. We were terribly worried about her, because she had been having awful problems and it had become a real fight trying to keep her in balance and out of the hospital. Since I was the one who prepared her meds all the time, I knew just how bad it was. Mom took twenty-seven meds a day. Even with all that, she kept on with her television show and she wrote a book, *Rainbow on a Hard Trail,* about her stroke and about Dad and how she was coping with his passing before her. She was a most remarkable individual.

After Dad's passing, Mom would say that she missed him so much and was ready to go as soon as the Lord would take her. But not just at that moment—she still had a few things she wanted to do. Of course, if would be all right if the Lord wanted her then; she just wished he'd hold off for a little while.

Recently, a gentleman approached me in the museum and asked me about the book Mom had been working on when she died. He wanted to know if she had finished enough of it to be published. He had heard Mom talking about it on *Date with*

Dale. It was a show on a religious network and her last appearance was on her Christmas show only about six weeks before she died. She started talking about this book she was working on. Well, she really wasn't working on one. As always, she had about three different ideas in development. They were not to be, even though they were all good ideas and she was very excited about all three of them. She was also writing lyrics for three or four new songs that remained unfinished when she died.

After his death, when interviewers would ask Mom what Dad had *really* been like, she took to saying that Dad had been like Popeye the Sailor: "I am what I am and that's all I am." Now, I don't think that's a good description of Dad at all. To a great extent, Dad was who you saw, but he was also a lot more complex than that. Dad didn't share his thoughts or emotions easily. In fact, I don't know that he shared them at all most of the time.

Mom's the one who was like Popeye. You knew exactly what she was thinking and feeling because she always told you. Sometimes she might take an opposite position in a discussion just to test you, to see how deeply you believed what you were saying. But by the end of the discussion, you were never in doubt about where she stood. The woman you saw on *Date with Dale* truly believed everything she said on that show. What she wrote about in her books were the people, issues, and things she cared truly about. Neither she nor Dad was a physically demonstrative, "huggy" person, but they loved their family and friends dearly. More important, they loved each other dearly.

Mom survived Dad by three years and kept herself busy and productive during that time, even though she missed him terribly every day. She often voiced her loneliness and seemed to enjoy going up to the cemetery to sit next to his grave and talk to him. She particularly loved to watch the sunset over the desert floor from the spot they chose to spend eternity. It was in the little things that I could see how much she missed him. Mom started eating the very things that she had teased him about or chided him for over the years. She had never really liked sardines and Dad loved them. All of a sudden she had to have sardines. She had never been a big egg eater. Now she wanted eggs all the time. If I asked her about the change, she would get very adamant that she had always loved these things. The little things can tell us so much.

Mom died surrounded by the family that loved her. We had been with her constantly for her last week and the last thing she heard were her kids and grandchildren singing her favorite hymns. It was the way she wanted to go.

Dad's funeral—or should I say funerals—was a nightmare. But three years later, Mom's funeral was a celebration. In fact, that's what she called it, "a celebration of my life." She told us not to grieve but instead be happy for her. After all, she had lived her life for that day. That did help put her death into perspective but, of course, it didn't keep us from grieving. After all, her gain was our loss. And our family will never be the same.

She had written her service herself—the whole thing. Mom had always been against wearing black at funerals. She preferred green for new life, but you could wear white. You could even wear red if you wanted to—anything but black. So for Mom's funeral, Dusty got the word out for the women not to wear black. Mom realized that a lot of the gentlemen wouldn't have a choice in the color of their suit so they could be excused!

Well, this young Baptist minister showed up in a black suit. And the first thing he said was, "Wouldn't you know everybody got the word but the Baptist." Mom would have loved that; she would have howled.

She had planned everything months, if not years, before. She had picked out her casket and had chosen just the perfect suit to go with its pink lining. Then she decided that she didn't like that casket, so she bought a new one. Then she had to buy a new dress because the pinks now clashed—you have to be color-coordinated, you know. She had written out the script for her service, picked every piece of music, and left Dusty detailed instructions of how and when she wanted everything done. She was in control even after her final breath.

So all in all, Mom's funeral was truly not an ordeal for us; it was filled with laughter and music, prayer and jubilation. I guess that pretty much sums up the way she lived her life—the way both Mom and Dad lived their lives.

They faced more heartbreak than two people should have known, but they were given enormous gifts of fame, accomplishment, and the love of their family. With the enduring high regard of their millions of fans, old and new, that adds up to a couple of significant, happy lives, the kind that any of us would be grateful to live. He was the King of the Cowboys and she was the Queen of the West. But they never acted like royalty—they were just plain Roy and Dale. And, more important to this Cowboy Princess, they were Mom and Dad.

Would I change anything if I could? I don't think so. It has been—and thank heaven still is—a great ride. I was given the most wonderful parents anyone could hope for—millions of other kids even prayed to be part of our family. Dad always made sure that I knew that he specifically chose me. And so, like Dad, I've always figured that I am exactly where I'm supposed to be. That day he appeared at Hope Cottage couldn't have been just a magnificent accident—it was meant to be.

I am just the extremely lucky little baby girl who reached up and grabbed his finger.

The End

References

Evans, Dale. "The Bible Tells Me So." Words and music by Dale Evans. © 1955 by Paramount–Roy Rogers Music Co., Inc.

———. "Happy Trails." Words and music by Dale Evans. © 1951, 1952 by Paramount–Roy Rogers Music Co., Inc.

George-Warren, Holly and Michelle Freedman. *How the West Was Worn.* Published in association with Autry Museum of Western Heritage, Los Angeles. (New York: Harry N. Abrams, 2001).

Green, Douglas R. *Singing in the Saddle.* (Nashville, TN: Vanderbilt University Press and Country Music Foundation Press, 2002).

Griffis, Ken. "Hear My Song." Copyright 1974, Rev. 1986.

O'Neal, Bill and Fred Goodwin. *The Sons of the Pioneers.* (Austin, TX: Eakin Press, 2001).

Rogers, Dale Evans. "Angel Unaware." Published and ©1953 Fleming H. Revell, Old Tappan, NJ.

———. "Dearest Debbie," Published and © 1965 Fleming H. Revell, Westwood, NJ.

———. "Salute to Sandy." Published and © 1967 Fleming H. Revell, Westwood, NJ.

Rogers, Roy and Dale Evans with Carlton Stowers. *Happy Trails: The Story of Roy Rogers and Dale Evans,* (Waco, TX: Word, Inc., 1979).